Y0-COR-709

You Can Survive the Corporate Culture

Bill Hendrickson

PublishAmerica
Baltimore

First printing

ISBN: 1-4137-3845-1
PUBLISHED BY PUBLISHAMERICA, LLLP
www.publishamerica.com
Baltimore

Printed in the United States of America

THIS BOOK IS DEDICATED WITH
LOVE, RESPECT, AND WONDER
TO THE MEMORY OF
CHARLIE BURROWS
WHO SURVIVED FOUR MERGERS, NUMEROUS
DOWN SIZINGS AND LAYOFFS,
THREATENED SPIN-OFFS, AND COUNTLESS
CHANGES IN MANAGEMENT UNTIL
HIS EARLY RETIREMENT.
SADLY, A REWARDING RETIREMENT ESCAPED HIM
AS HE FELL VICTIM TO
ALS (LOU GEHRIG'S DISEASE) AND
COULD NOT SURVIVE ITS RAVAGES.
SURVIVAL IS NOT ALWAYS ASSURED.

ACKNOWLEDGMENTS

A book like this could not have been written without the cooperation of many individuals: some who gave encouragement, some who gave valued advice, and many others who subjected themselves to interviews from which the stories of survival, or otherwise, were taken to fill these chapters.

Many of these folks have titles and/or advanced academic degrees, but for the purposes of these acknowledgments, we will list them by name only. They all played significant roles in the preparation of this book and some had direct influence during my working years with my own survival—or the lack thereof.

All my helpers include Ken Petersen, Jack Rockett, Ed Pringle, Pam Hendrickson, Web Lewis, Marc Maffey, Lisa Hendrickson, Jana Mundey, Doug Hendrickson, Kevin Sowers, Debbie Gulino, Laura Feather, Doug Sherwen, Laurie Sherwen, Lauren McGlynn, Bob Otterbourg, Marlene Jupiter, Margaret Lawson, Milan Pham, Bill Gulino, Felix Hendrickson, Gerial Thornburg-May, Steve May, Keith Feather, John Wagner, and of course my wife—and loving critic—Sally Feather Hendrickson.

Then there were others who influenced some of the experiences related in the book, but know nothing about this literary effort and who might or might not recognize the incidents where they had influence. These include Bill Gilroy, Gordon Crosby, Harold Hook, Kip Kirby, David Griffith, Larry Corroon, Richard Broughton, Barbara Gruber, Lud Kapusta, Peter Wilke, Lenora Miller, Susan Jay, Fran Auerbach, Fred Becher, Warren Smith, Buck Tilson, Crawford Black, Bob Corroon, Jim Ross, Ron Kumin, Clare Zalud, and others whose names should remain anonymous. But as anyone looks back, there will have been a large cast of persons who had influence on their lives—some we would gladly have avoided, others we cherish.

Table of Contents

PREFACE

You know those familiar film and television ads: "This movie you must see" or "don't miss the opening episode of the new season's highly-acclaimed TV drama series" (that most likely was scratched after six weeks due to the ratings that were never there). We'd like to think that this book is a MUST READ! Why? Because everyone working in any environment with more than one person is immersed into some kind of culture, and in order to survive where one is now or where one plans to be, the message within the covers of this book will be your road map, your guide book, your easy-to-read survival instructions. If you're presently employed, as you read along, you'll be nodding your head: "Exactly what I found" or, "Just like it is every day at the shop." Or, if you're new in the job market, you'll be picking up tips about what to avoid and what to look forward to. Just like the pollen in the air which interferes with proper, comfortable, and healthy breathing, many elements of the corporate culture interfere with our job performance causing it to be uncomfortable and perhaps even unhealthful.

Every element of human society has a culture. You might not think of it this way, but every home, no matter the physical structure, the location, or the number of inhabitants, has its own special culture.

The people living there create the culture. Every public park, all theaters, churches, physicians' offices, restaurants, non-profit institutions, suburban neighborhoods have their own culture and environment that might have been carefully crafted and maintained or that might have evolved over some period of time without any predetermination. It's not only the architecture, the design, the location, or even the smells that help create the culture. Those passing through, working, playing, eating, cooking, or what have you, create the bulk of the culture. You can sense a culture as you enter a building or even as you venture into a yard or garden. You won't know exactly of what the culture consists, but you'll know there is an attitude, a style, a sense of identity in each environment you enter. At least four of your senses will all be reaching out their antennae to bring you a visual, auditory, olfactory, and tactile reading of the environment you have entered. And with these preliminary pieces of data you then can begin to make some rudimentary judgments about the folks whose imprint created this environment.

The culture in all venues is the overall atmosphere of all the elements blended together within the surroundings. A home, no matter its size, type of building or otherwise, including the number of persons living there, as well as conditions of cleanliness, tidiness, and the personal attitudes of the inhabitants, etc., has a distinctive culture. And because those living there do so in mostly intimate, open, and continuing relationships one with the others, survival in the home culture is well understood and well managed by many of us. Before you say it, we know, unfortunately, there are too many homes where the culture is anything but stable—abuse, poverty, pending divorces, hurtful addictions, and many unpleasant and disturbing influences can explode the culture of a home. But by and large, most individuals within a home have learned how to move about in a safe and sane cultural environment.

But workplaces, particularly in large corporations or institutions, have cultures that can set off every warning bell within our beings and send some of us running to therapists or, in a last resort, running for the door. Sometimes these cultures are almost impossible to fathom because of the multiple pressures within the institutional environment. And along with all these pressures, the players regularly change within the institutional world and these personnel changes will always bring modifications to the existing culture—some which you may support and welcome, others which send you back to the couch or out the door.

The higher ups in the parent organization may have a defined mission along with strategic plans to guide the ship of state, but as divisions, departments, sections, units, etc. implement all the grand stuff, the culture of each separate entity has a major impact on the goals, results, and total success or failure of the organization. Like the Tonawanda Towel Manufacturing Corporation, for example: the Board of Directors, the CEO, and the Marketing Vice President all decided *in unison*, and without consultation with the production staff, to add a new and highly-recommended strengthening starch to their paper towels which would allow them to advertise their product as the toughest towel on the super market shelves. But wait a minute! The department foreman and the team in the shop where the towels were produced were paid on an incentive compensation basis, primarily based on a strict expense budget and they knew that adding this strengthening element to the product would add manufacturing costs and would blow the budget and their beloved production bonuses.

So, knowing all the techniques and tricks of manufacturing paper towels, the team was able to produce Tonawanda Towels that looked and felt tougher than the competition, but actually were no tougher than the product manufactured using the old manufacturing formula prior to the recommended addition of senior management's high-cost supplement. The culture of the production team was strongly influenced by the compensation package, so much so that even the directions from senior management could be ignored by the team's secretly creative, but mutinous, unison action.

Therefore, in this case, senior management's mission and strategy had been scuttled by another culture down the line. We'll find out later how these competing cultures affect the mother ship. This example, however, is proof enough that organizations frequently have multiple cultures which can be mutually competitive. There's a heavy risk, of course, when orders from upstairs are ignored and actually twisted to give the appearance of obedience, and subverted to protect a compensation arrangement on behalf of the mutineers.

Those who labor in these large organizations in order to survive the push and pull of their surroundings must learn how to swim in the very turbulent waters of corporate rapids. And if organizations are to prosper, management from the top down must understand the multiple cultures throughout and must give encouragement to those who are the culture survivors. This encouragement should be manifested in higher earnings, more rapid advancement, and overall greater opportunities for growth and satisfaction. The survivors will not only prosper personally, but the parent organization will also see more satisfactory results that will please their constituents. That's what we'll be trying to do in this book: laying out the manner in which all can manage and survive within their various corporate cultures. Survival is the first priority of institutional existence. Everything is a lot easier once that is mastered.

Keep in mind that the corporate and institutional cultures are person made and you as a person have at least an even chance to survive by reading this book and becoming aware of the situations as they are presented. As you study the various chapters that might have meaning for you in your present situation, or that might have applied to a previous employment encounter, remember that often the *best* you can do is survive. You might never find a totally satisfactory blending of who you are with the culture you are, or were, in. There is no perfect solution. As you might also have learned by now, there is no such thing as perfection in any element of your life. One person's perfection is another's nemesis. But as you learn to survive, your life will be more comfortable and you will develop a strong sense of security as you practice your trade within the corporate culture.

CHAPTER ONE

WELCOME

Before we plunge into our study of corporate culture and how various cultures impact you and, more important, the reverse, how you can impact a culture, you obviously need to have a job, start working, and be welcomed into the arms of your employment culture. In this chapter we'll review some samples of conditions people have found upon entering a new culture and we will taste some anxiety levels felt by some as they accepted new jobs and faced new and unknown cultures. We will also lay out simple, but important, guidelines to follow during the welcoming process that will assure you more comfort and greater acceptance into whatever the new culture has in store. Come along now as we get welcomed into the world of work—whether it's the first time for you or repeat of several employment adventures.

There are dozens of ways one is welcomed into a new job, position, or situation— no matter what you call it. It depends upon who you are, where you will be working, what level your position is, what kind of organization you will be with, and many other factors we don't need to mention right here. Let me tell you about a welcome

BILL HENDRICKSON

I received at a middle-sized New York City company many years ago.

I was to be employed as a mid-level executive, running a small department. I had been insistently and incessantly recruited for more than one year by the Chief Operating Officer of the company. I finally agreed to their terms, became revved up about this new grand opportunity in the big city, moved my family from Buffalo, New York to a commuting suburb of New York City and plunged right in. Well, the first day on the job, another new executive and I were invited to a lovely catered lunch in the company board room (I still remember the tasty lobster tails) where we were entertained along with the COO (the CEO was in the hospital at the time, never returned to work, and ultimately died), the Chief Financial Officer, the Chief Legal Officer, and the senior officers of several operating departments. What a welcome! Good cheer, lots of warm, welcoming comments, and smiles all around. Little did I know, however, that both senior officers above me in the department I was to manage were in the process of being canned. The COO wanted a complete change. One of the two officers was to be immediately made a kind of "emeritus" and the other was to be shifted to a less important position which sadly destroyed his spirit. He eventually left the company for another job, and after a few unsatisfactory years there, suffered an early death.

The fact was, that without my having been told during the interview process, I actually had been hired to replace both gentlemen whom I thought were to have been my superiors, both whom had interviewed me and encouraged me to accept the job, and both, unknown to them, were on their way out!

What a welcome. The warm and hearty welcome in the company board room turned into sabotage for two other long term, and generally respected, employees of the company. Their only problem was that the COO wanted a clean sweep and, while I was not the broom, I provided the surface on which the broom whisked two individuals off the sidewalk and into the ditch.

That whole welcoming process with the surprises that followed, proved quickly, but too late, two critical and essential truths to be learned before beginning a new position: 1) do thorough research about the job, the people, the reputation of those interviewing you, and the health of the organization in which you will be working, and 2) be prepared for surprises that are bound to appear no matter how thorough your pre-employment research. (See Chapter Four) The firm from which I had come was widely known and respected for having a well-designed management philosophy and structure, along with a history of carefully crafted practices and procedures. I was familiar with its culture and foolish enough to assume that since both firms were in the same industry, the cultures would match. Wrong! I was so taken with my new job and my move to New York City (a move which I had coveted for many years) that I was hardly prepared for this new culture at the new company and a new management style which I now call "management by intrigue."

As you can imagine, there are numerous ways a welcome can be arranged for any job. New Chief Executives of large organizations receive media attention, lots of bells and whistles, often fat employment and post-employment contracts, with speeches and letters of congratulations all around. New trainees in the bond department of a securities firm are barely welcomed and hardly noticed. But for any level position, the first few days of employment during the welcoming process are critical and are the times when you can make the all important "first impression" and where the employer can give you the lay of the land and hopefully make you feel comfortable.

There won't be many lobster tail lunches in the corporate board room in the usual welcoming process. No matter what the welcoming process, please keep in mind that the type of welcome you receive is much less important than your own personal attitude toward the job you are about to begin.

Therefore, as you begin this book, the most essential advice to remember is that you are bringing yourself into this new position, carrying along in your personal luggage, your education, your family heritage, your past employment experience, if any, and other critical matters that make up YOU. As you'll learn in chapter after chapter in this book, the YOU element will always be the primary key— sometimes the only key—to culture survival. Before you are swallowed up in this new culture, you will have swum in other cultures that may or may not have prepared you for this new venture. While this book is to provide revelations on surviving in most any culture situations, it's a good idea for us now to focus briefly on some of the luggage you might be carrying as you glide through the revolving doors of your new world. And be sure to remember that this culture will, in fact, be your world. Time spent on the job, next to sleeping time for most people, makes up the major active part of any day, so, the time spent "on the job" is really and truly your world. So actually, what *is* in that shopping bag of experience you are carefully shepherding up the steps, into the elevator, and through the main entrance to your new life?

To set the stage, here are some hypothetical examples of several fictitious individuals as they entered new employment. We'll focus on their levels of anticipation and anxiety as they moved from one job to another, or as they first entered the work force and faced a world of unknown experiences.

SITUATION ONE—EXPERIENCED PERSON: A man accepted a new job, in a familiar industry based on past experience, with expectations of minor cultural differences compared to past employment. His familiarity with his industry and with the expected culture of his new employer made his job switch anxiety proof.

SITUATION TWO— EXPERIENCED WOMAN, NEW JOB, NEW LOCATION: A young woman accepted a new job, moved to a new city, and had no friends except those to be found in the new job. Similar industry, but with a new employer and a new location, so there were some cultural concerns and moderate anxiety. The anxiety she experienced resulted more from finding her way around a new city; finding housing; and becoming part of a new, urban world. The welcome she received from her new associates was a strong indication of what to expect in the cultural mix of her new employer. She brought a good work record with her, so that helped her to become accepted in the new culture, assuming she was not considered a threat by any of her new associates.

SITUATION THREE—YOUNG GRADUATE, FIRST "REAL" JOB: A young and green fellow, just out of school (high school or college), took a new job, possibly the first one that came along, and was totally naïve as to what type of culture to expect. In fact, the word "culture" had never crossed his mind. Waiting table, mowing lawns, supermarket check out clerk, camp jobs, back packing in the mountains, etc. had provided little experience for a "real" job, so the high level of anticipation overcame any anxiety he might have had. He didn't have enough work experience to know how to anticipate culture or be prepared to deal with it. Naiveté sometimes is the wonder drug that helps control anxiety.

SITUATION THREE—MIDDLE-AGED WIDOW, RE-ENTERING WORK WORLD: A recently widowed woman re-entered the work world after 25 years of motherhood and managing a home, family, and community volunteer projects. She was very fearful of the modern working life after hearing mostly unfounded rumors and gossip of today's work environment and culture. She was highly anxious and nervous, but needed to plunge in both for extra income as well as renewed adult companionship. She was on the lookout for hidden shoals and other unknown dangers, most of which, she would realize later, were imagined. In many situations such as this, the arrival of an older person into an existing group of more youthful employees adds warmth, maturity, and increased stability.

SITUATION FOUR—WOMAN MANAGER, JADED AND SUSPICIOUS, CHANGES JOBS: A woman left a middle-management job where company politics interfered heavily with her best efforts. Her former boss was crafty, devious, and able to obtain favors for himself from senior management at the expense of others, mostly innocent staffers. She accepted a new job in a similar industry with cautious anxiety and some hopes that history would not be repeated in the new culture. She was very cautious and wary and entered the new employment with antennae on alert. Her intolerable past experience had alerted her so that she could gauge the new culture rather quickly and easily sense whether history was, in fact, to be repeated.

SITUATION FIVE—YOUNG, RURAL GRADUATE; NEW JOB; AND URBAN ENVIRONMENT: A recent college graduate moved into big city life with new employment after having spent his youth in mostly rural surroundings. He had a college degree from the "in state" university. No question about it, the culture of Chicago, Dallas, New York, or Los Angeles or even Cincinnati, Charlotte, or Jacksonville would differ markedly from Ashe County, North Carolina. Yes, the *urban culture* can be managed and dealt with. Many young people move into the cities and survive with lots of help from their peers, but the *work site culture* could be another story. The culture on the job would need to be studied and understood quickly no matter how comforting the welcome. The folks back in Ashe County offered large helpings of fearsome advice about life in the big city, but once actually in the city and working at the new job, our young country boy would need to quickly adjust to multiple new cultures. These would include urban housing, urban shopping, urban transportation, competitive work sites, mixed ages and genders at work, new performance requirements, and a host of other urban and work site cultures. Based on a dramatically changed living environment and a vast amount of inexperience, this young man approached his new employment with a high level of anxiety.

These brief and fictitious summaries of fear, anticipation, and personal histories could fill hundreds of pages in this book since every person brings his/her own past into the present condition. As you read the chapters ahead you will need to keep clearly in mind your own history as it might relate to your new position. More than you expect, it will be this history that you will call upon to help you survive in the corporate world.

I encourage you, even at this very moment, put this book aside temporarily and mentally scan some of the signposts from your past that have helped shape who you are today. Some of these reminiscences may bring painful memories. Others will bring visions of more joyous experiences.

As you are doing this recall exercise, you will also hear in your mind the words of teachers, family members, rivals, and close friends that can give you some lifelines into whatever this new venture holds. Listen and sort out what strengths your personal history will offer and keep them up front in your mind (or better yet, jot them down on paper or in your PC) for use when called upon. You're never too advanced in your life to ignore the past. As you move from one experience of life into the next, your past continues to grow and will provide increasing guidance to shape your present and your future. The past is the most essential element in guiding you through the present and into the future.

We'll pursue the welcoming process a bit further. Let's assume for purposes of this discussion of welcomes, that you have been hired for a mid-level position in the marketing department of a financial institution. You are known to have good creative writing skills. You prepared for this career in school, and have had helpful experience in a previous job. You fully anticipate no culture shocks. You've probably been in the building in several different locations during the pre-employment interview process, so the surroundings are familiar. But, still, you haven't toured the whole place and you have no idea what the working conditions will be in the specific area of your work.

As a part of your own personal welcoming process, you need to immediately begin to make mental notes of the new environment you are entering. Do you recall seeing World War II movies and watching the infantry soldiers enter a recently liberated village in France or Germany? Whether riding a truck or a tank or walking through the narrow streets, the soldiers would be wary, looking out for stray snipers, and being extraordinarily careful to avoid booby traps or land mines. While your job is not to "liberate" any territory, you need to be alert and sensitive to the conditions of your new surroundings. You can begin to get a sense of the culture of your new employer as you are escorted to your new work area.

The first and most obvious viewing will be the actual conditions of the building—the furniture, the paint on the walls, the floor covering, and anything that can give you a sense of the quality of care given to the organization by the employees and the management. You can glance into offices or cubicles, look at the conditions of the labs or the manufacturing floors, and make a visual check of health and safety conditions. Even more to the point, you can make a quick assessment of the work habits of visible staffers. I recently visited a small suite of offices housing a staff in a department of the county government. I happened to know that the morale of this staff was in steep decline and the appearance of the work site showed a general lack of care and upkeep. More shocking, this was a department whose main purpose was to greet and serve the public. The maintenance condition of this department likely indicated the staff's capability of performing their service effectively. As a new employee here, what should be your immediate reaction? You should be wary, harbor some suspicion, and maintain a high level of alertness as you start your new job. The first few days on any job will give you a broad overview of what's ahead in the realm of corporate culture, but even with warning signs, don't begin to make early and rash judgments from these superficial findings. File away what you have just observed. You'll learn soon enough about the true culture in the organization. These first impressions are just that— impressions.

More important than the physical conditions of the place will be your early introductions to those with whom you will be working— your supervisor, your closest associates, and those for whom you will be doing your creative writing. As you are introduced to your new associates, there is one essential element in your own personality that I will insist upon: LET YOURSELF BE

VULNERABLE! Why, on earth, do you want me to become vulnerable, you ask? Isn't vulnerability a big risk? Won't I be taken advantage of if these new folks realize my vulnerability? Won't predators pounce? The answers are yes, yes, and yes.

Let me explain how this openness and apparent vulnerability immediately gives you an edge in the getting acquainted process. First and foremost, you have exhibited vulnerability intentionally. You are not a babe in the woods, a wide-eyed innocent ready and willing to please anyone and everyone. You have displayed an openness, some personal warmth, and by these gestures of goodwill your new associates will immediately feel comfortable with you. That's what I mean by vulnerability. This style of openness will tend to put people at ease in a "get acquainted" situation. They'll let their curiosity and possible suspicion of the "new guy in town behavior" gradually melt away, giving you a strategic advantage and allow you early on, to get to know who these people really are.

Possibly you're unaccustomed to exhibiting vulnerability. You might have been told all your life to be tight—keep your guard up—be prepared to strike back if necessary. All these defenses will be much easier to implement if needed, assuming you have shown this vulnerability early on and gained a degree of confidence from your associates. Therefore, if you need some protection or defense as your work progresses, the confidence others have in you from this early vulnerability will give you some power and strength to withstand difficult or negative conditions that might befall you.

Expressing your vulnerability is not difficult. With these several obvious and rather simple tips to smooth your way into early confidence of the new associates you'll begin to fit into the environment and the culture sooner and more comfortably. These are tips to be used not only in the job situation, but in many places and situations in your life when encountering people who don't know you from Adam or Eve.

• Dress comfortably in clothes not intended to make a statement of who you are and what your interests are; don't display what some would feel is excessive body ornamentation.

• Repeat the names of those to whom you are introduced and try to shake all hands at the time of the introductions.

• Keep an attitude of good humor. Don't, by all means, crack any jokes, but exhibit an attitude of cheerfulness. That means smiles and laughter at the appropriate moments.

• Look you new associates directly in the eyes. Nothing is worse than a conversation where one of the participants is glancing off into another world and you are stuck looking at someone's ear lobe or shirt collar. If your eyes are on them, they will more likely begin to feel that you are trustworthy and not a potential threat. Eye contact means trust. You need to remember throughout this process of becoming acquainted with your new employer, your associates, and the total environment, that your number one objective in these early days is to gain the confidence of those around you. With this confidence your work will commence smoothly and you will not be troubled with difficult inter-personal relationships.

During these introductory moments, exhibit a genuine interest toward what you are being shown, to whom you are being introduced, and to the general surroundings.

Do not—REPEAT—do not immediately and audibly compare your new place, or people, or overall environment with any situation from the past. These unnecessary comparisons, if stated, will label you as a whiner, a malcontent, or as someone trying to impress. It's a waste and a blotch on your efforts to be accepted by your new buddies. Just don't do it. As best you can, make like these work conditions and these new associates are what you had hoped they would be. Maybe they are and maybe they aren't. There will be plenty of time to blend into the new conditions and attempt to make alterations, if needed. This may sound like your Mother talking, but show sincerity in your approval of the overall new situation. The longer you are in any job, it becomes your reality. You will face many issues and a few surprises as you move into your position and commence the work for which you have been hired. Be wary, be open, and put all your effort into superior performance of the work for which you were hired.

Your welcoming process now has been completed and you are ready to become part of the corporate culture.

LESSON I: When you embark on new employment, be very alert to all your surroundings. Do not make and announce early judgments. Allow yourself to be carefully vulnerable until you sort out who's who among your new companions.

Remember that who you are now is the result of your personal history. Exhibit the best of this history into any new job situation and your welcome will be smooth and supportive.

CHAPTER TWO

CULTURE, BY DEFINITION

Culture. Is it an attitude? Is it a life style? Is it a high level of being civilized? Just what is it, and how is culture a factor in the corporate existence?

There are multiple definitions of culture, many with similarities, others unrelated to sister definitions. We'll look at a few found in *Merriam Webster's Collegiate Dictionary, 10th Edition.* Among the examples found in this edition of *Webster's*, which relate culture to aesthetic aspects of society, the definitions are "enlightenment and excellence of taste acquired by intellectual and aesthetic training;" and "acquaintance with and taste in fine arts, humanities, and broad aspects of science as distinguished from vocational and technical skills."

Another very broad definition favored by the anthropologists and encompassing wide elements of humanity, defines culture as "the integrated pattern of human knowledge, belief, and behavior that depends upon man's capacity for learning and transmitting knowledge to succeeding generations." With this definition we can reach back into unrecorded human history to appreciate and understand culture as it developed, reoriented itself, and swept across all human existence into today's world.

If any of you readers have studied biology or zoology in school or college, you'll be familiar with this definition of culture: "cultivation of living material in prepared nutrient media." If you remember, this is where you put some bacterial material in a protein culture in a petri dish to study its growth. This book is not a replay of your school science class.

More specific to this book is a particular *Webster* definition that says "the set of shared attitudes, values, goals, and practices that characterizes a company or corporation," and I might add, "a governmental, cultural, educational or not-for-profit institution."

There are other definitions of this same word, and, as we all may say, "that's one of the complexities of the English language." One word may be burdened with multiple definitions. One phrase may have a word or even an inflection which gives it an entirely different meaning from the same word with a different inflection. If we've grown up with all these variables, so much the better. But if we've emigrated from a far off land, English can be troublesome, frustrating, and most difficult to master. And with a word like "culture" with multiple definitions, who knows how the poor immigrant will navigate the English language.

In this book, we're planning to focus on the many attitudes and practices that form the culture within a variety of organizations. There may be many job situations where the culture is nurturing, congenial, and very supporting. During the many interviews I have conducted with a great number of individuals, I found many who had spent at least some of their working years in the comfort zone of supportive culture. They may have moved on to another position in the same or different organization and been faced with a hostile or selfish culture. They may have actually remained at the same job, at the same desk or machine, in the same department or on the same team, and had the culture change around them! When the culture changes to the disadvantage of employees, it can be unsettling, to say the least, or even disastrous in the extreme. Such dramatic upheavals are often caused by changes in management, mergers, declining fortunes of the organization, or a host of other apparent and potentially negative occurrences.

As we discussed in the first chapter, entering a job situation throws everyone into a fully established culture. Most people have very little insight into what they will find upon arrival. Many of us never bothered to inquire as to the quality of the culture we were stepping into. Probably most of us didn't even consider the word "culture" when we were applying, being interviewed, or exploring a job situation. We wanted or needed the position, may have studied long and hard for this spot in our career, and had given little or no thought to what we might have found in the sense of culture upon arrival. That's exactly why everyone needs to follow the suggestions in Chapter One upon job arrival.

What now follows are two graphic examples of culture—one, within an entire nationwide industry and the other, within a small local organization. In both these examples, the culture that had existed changed dramatically and completely, resulting from conditions that changed both within and outside the organizations.

In the first example, a specific brand of culture had been painstakingly nurtured down to the last nut and bolt over decades within a certain industry and corporation—the telephone industry as represented by that monster of a company, AT & T. We'll see later how this agonizingly tailored culture exploded into wildly different components when the structure of the industry was shaken with the force of a Richter shattering earthquake.

Historically, the American Telephone and Telegraph Company was established in 1885 as a subsidiary of the American Bell Telephone Company, Alexander Graham Bell's company that had been founded earlier to supply telephone instruments to Bell-licensed phone companies across the United States. During the last decade of the nineteenth century, many independent telephone companies were formed after Mr. Bell's patents expired. But by that time, the giant AT & T had a huge swath of the business and over the years developed and owned large regional phone companies known then as New York Telephone, Ohio Bell Telephone, Illinois Bell, etc. These companies all operated with the same cultural tenets, namely:

• Service to the customers
• Controlled pricing among the local companies and through the parent;
• Identically and fully-trained technicians, marketing staff, and administrators;
• Complete ownership by the company of all equipment that had been installed in a customer's premises;
• Loyalty among the employees to their employer and almost lifetime guarantees of jobs for anyone who chose "telephone" as a career;
• Total duplication of products, ideals, and services throughout the vast system so that an employee moving from one Bell company to another would always feel at home and would know all the work procedures. Identical culture throughout the entire system.

Early in my working life I spent one year at the Ohio Bell Telephone Company in Cleveland, Ohio. I was a marketing person and drove a dull, olive green Bell company car to visit small business customers. Every Bell employee who wasn't driving a service truck drove the exact same model and color car. During all my telephone training I was even instructed where to place my hands on the car's steering wheel while driving in order to provide me the most comfort and safety! That was too much. I left after one year, so steeped and smothered in Bell system rigid culture that I wondered if I had not returned to the U.S. Army, my most immediate previous, and also very rigid, employer.

Within the confines of Bell territory, no one had to sell customers on using a Bell company phone or equipment. In most large cities, and in many small communities and in rural areas, the Bell company was the only phone game in town. There was no competition! AT & T was a nationwide monopoly with an overriding culture that was well known even to many Americans who had never worked for the company. Everyone in America knew someone who had worked or was working for a Bell company. The attitudes and culture of "Ma Bell," as the whole system had been christened, were widely known and accepted by the majority of Americans.

In 1934, President Franklin D. Roosevelt signed the Communications Act which brought interstate telephone businesses under the regulation of the Federal Communications Commission (FCC). This allowed the federal government to have more control of the telephone industry, and to focus on this giant monopoly, AT & T. After several failed attempts to fracture the system, a federal court approved a consent decree in 1982 which suddenly, finally, and permanently broke up the Bell System into local and long distance companies. AT & T itself retained the long distance charter and seven "Baby Bells," as they were nicknamed, provided the local service covering the territories previously managed by the various regional 22 local Bell companies.

What does all this have to do with corporate culture, you ask? The most direct and obvious answer is that all of a sudden there was an explosion of competition unequaled by any previous industrial or corporate divorce action. Other companies such as MCI and General Telephone (now Sprint) could now sell local service as well as long distance service to the phoning public within the old Bell territories. Many other "start-up" telephone companies hit the lines running to compete with AT & T and the other new "Baby Bells." And as time went by, these seven offspring were squalling like spoiled children and were competing with one another and eventually were competing with their harassed former mother for various portions of the market once held exclusively by one or another member of this fractured family. New companies and their aggressive management and employees started muscling into each others' services and territories. Price wars abounded. Individual phone users were bombarded by solicitations to change companies, change service, and dump the old Bell connections.

The steady, comfortably conforming, well-rehearsed, and well-remembered Bell culture was ravaged by rival pugnacious, often aggravating, cultures founded and funded by sometimes wild entrepreneurs who aggressively fought for the Bell business and who had employees eager to upset the Bell apple cart and walk away with all the good apples. Carefully controlled prices were trashed by the upstarts so much so that the financial stability of several of the Bell companies was shaken and several of these new, aggressive giants of the telecommunications industry slid into bankruptcy or even disappeared.

This aggressive, cost cutting, sales driven culture in the new telephone marketplace would never have been remotely thought of within the historic Bell System. Many of the long-time Bell employees sought refuge in early retirement due to the sudden change in working conditions. They were professionally horrified at some of the tactics displayed by the new breed of telephone managers. They felt their best course of action was to quietly fade away and enjoy the solid pension earned by many years of uneventful, but stable, employment within the old Bell System.

Now we'll make an abrupt switch from a "macro" to a "micro" culture change that recently happened—all for the better—at a health and fitness center in my neighborhood. This well-equipped facility includes an Olympic size swimming pool as well as exercise and kiddie pools, a professional size hockey and artistic ice rink, along with two cardio-fitness machine and weight rooms, snack bar, tanning bed, massage room, rooms for aerobic and yoga sessions, showers, lockers, and a small equipment sales nook. All this was created from the dream of a local resident who talked the county government into putting up some of the money. In addition, a major old line New England conservative mutual fund investment company made a significant investment to build and staff this much needed physical haven in a semi-rural, but fast developing, community.

Getting the place going wasn't all that tough: people in the area craved such a health spot, but finding enough members to carry the debt load owed the investment company became an ever growing burden. The fitness management company that had been contracted to operate the center had difficulty finding appropriate staff; had trouble building a satisfactory culture within the organization; and had further trouble with salaries, benefits, and other employment issues. The interest payments to the investor were missed and they were forced to foreclose on their investment. However, as a credit to the investor's thoughtful management, they allowed that the center continue to operate.

A new management team was brought in and the county continued to pay its annual contribution that allowed operations to continue. The disgruntled staff welcomed a planned change in management groups, and hoped for a quick improvement in the existing depressed culture. The new team installed a new dynamic leader and additional staff was brought on board to greatly enhance the services offered to the exercising public. With the new management, the total atmosphere of the center changed dramatically. In other words, there was a culture exchange. The original management that was around at the birth of the place had begun to tire. Worse, they had to initiate austere programs to keep the place alive as they saw the finances dwindle toward the threat of dissolution. The new management, having been brought in to create a new culture environment, did just that. They saw the commitment of the original mutual fund investor and saw that the county government planned to continue its annual contribution, so they came onto the scene when the air was clear and all the signals were in "go" position. A new education director was employed who created more family activities, started health and wellness classes, developed team building, and breathed new energy into the existing programs. Some of the facilities were modified more toward the members' needs and wishes, and, overall, a positive, easy-to-live with culture was created. This gave each staff member not only fewer sleepless nights, but an eagerness to show up for work and promote the positive welfare of the complex. That is what a wholesale culture exchange can do for an organization.

And what did this change in the culture accomplish? Here's a list of results:

• More new members, including full family memberships, that created additional revenue for the facility;
• A completely positive attitude among all staff;
• Improvement in the overall appearance and cleanliness of the center;
• More local publicity promoting the center's programs;
• Easier recruitment of better qualified and more highly trained fitness personnel.

The culture revolution created by the breakup of the entire Bell telephone system has had an earth shaking, and some say devastating, impact on American telecommunications. It will continue to affect the lives, the communications habits, and the pocket books of all phoning Americans *for as long as we use telephones!* Never has there been such a general corporate revolution of culture coming from one single instant decision. All Americans have been affected. On the local level, the culture exchange at the Triangle Sportsplex impacted the lives of the few, now satisfied, employees and all of the appreciative members.

These are two completely different, and quite extreme, examples of how corporate culture affects both the institutions and those depending on the institutions for service and support. An organization's culture impacts not only employees within the organizations, but all those in any way related to the products or services of the organization.

As you settle into a place of employment, you most likely won't be faced with the titanic explosion of a Bell system upheaval nor perhaps even a wholesale turnaround of culture similar to that of the Sportsplex. But you can be assured without question—there will be a culture bubbling along in your new environment and, good or bad, you'll be living with it on a daily, minute-by-minute basis. All of this need not worry nor alarm you. Please remember, you have a responsibility to yourself to begin to understand this culture. As time goes by and the longer you are employed in one position, you will have increasing opportunities to effect culture changes which will improve working conditions for both you and your associates. But don't rush it!

LESSON II: Accept the culture of the organization of which you are a part and learn as much about this culture (history, past and present leaders, and conditions that have led to culture changes in the past). Do not attempt to influence culture changes until you have established credibility and formed some alliances.

CHAPTER THREE

WHAT'S EXPECTED OF YOU

At the time this book was being written, computer technology had rapidly been controlling a commanding majority of work site activities—in clerical business operations, automobile building, home construction, hospital management, book publishing—in nearly 100% of everything we deal with on a 24 hour basis. So, listen to this, "How familiar are you with the technology required in this job we are discussing?" That very often is one of the first questions posed to you during your pre-employment interviews—even before the job was to have been offered. If the pre-employment interviews had been conducted professionally, that question would have been both asked *and* answered before any job had been offered.

But how many pre-employment interviews are conducted professionally? In one small non-profit organization with which I am familiar, many of the paid staff moved up from prior work as volunteers and, with an interest in the mission and the work of the non-profit, floated to the top of the pond when a new paid person was needed. Rarely was there a full fledged and professional pre-employment interview. References were rarely checked. The former volunteer—now paid employee—was never given the opportunity of knowing what exactly was expected in their job. Likewise, often this non-profit had no pre-determined set of expectations for the new person, now receiving a salary. My advice to the management of the organization was to stop employing "walk-ons" and to use a more professional pre-employment procedure. Walk-ons, as you know in the competitive world of college athletics, are those who do not qualify athletically for a sports scholarship, but are allowed on the team to assist in practice sessions and to occasionally take part in a one-sided regular game. But they never rise up to "paid" (athletic scholarship) status.

So it should be when becoming employed. All the obvious technical and personal job requirements should be clearly explained during the pre-employment process so that when one actually is on the job, *one will, without question, know what's expected of them.*

A full understanding of job expectations is critical no matter who you are, what the job is, where you fit into the organization's hierarchy, what you will be paid, what perks you might be offered, and on and on. A new chief executive needs to know what's expected in that senior position and so does an entry-level programmer trainee in a technology company.

Knowing the expectations of those who employed you is one of the most essential elements of anyone landing a new position or job. Sadly, too many people approach a new job knowing only superficially what the expectations are for their performance. Without knowing these expectations, they begin to stumble, sometimes even on the first day of work. It is absolutely rule number one that when you take a position you know full well what is expected of you and that *you perform from Day One up to the full expectations of those who employed you.*

A good example is the extremely competitive world of advertising. People often are hired for their creative abilities— cartooning, writing, musical talent, marketing, or other talents which exhibit creativity. Immediately upon being employed, because of their experience and qualifications, they quickly plunge into assignments which may, or may not, be what they had expected. If the talent of the new person doesn't mesh with the expectations of the agency, trouble will quickly brew, and without much fanfare, the new person will either be relegated to a non-essential spot in the agency or ushered out. Survival here is totally wrapped around performing up to expectations.

Knowing what's expected of you and performing up to expectations is essential for you to blend into your new culture. I once was recruited and employed by a large consulting agency in New York. The person who recruited and hired me happened to be the brother of the company president. Otherwise, according to those who knew him, only through this blood relationship would he himself be working there. Anyway, I was hired to manage a small department of about seven people. I was to motivate them to produce new business. I was expected to provide good service and maintain solid relations with clients. It was anticipated that through my management, the department would grow and prosper. Further, I was expected to develop cooperative relationships with other departments in the company and work with them for the common good of the organization.

WELL! The person who employed me, unfortunately, received very limited respect from the folks in the other departments. They didn't understand his methods and generally downgraded his intelligence. When I arrived on the job, eager to perform according to expectations, I had no inkling that the man who hired me was so maligned by others in the organization. The fact that I would be working for this man made me immediately suspect for even accepting a job offered by this yo-yo. One of the expectations my new boss had given me was to "work well with other departments." With this one expectation I met the Great Wall of China.

Another set of expectations given me by this lowly-regarded boss was the management and motivation of my own departmental staff. Shortly after I started work, the expectations switched and I was given the ominous task of firing at least two of the staff members! They were unqualified for the job, he had said. They were impossible to train and motivate, I was told. They needed to be replaced. All this bit of skullduggery came after I was on the job. Like a good soldier, I terminated two of the existing staff and went out into the market place to find replacements.

As I said above, my initial expectations were to manage and motivate these staff persons. After not so much as a day on the job, the signals had been switched toward rapid termination and immediate replacement. Replacements came, but slowly, since "the street" had a pretty good fix on the reputation of my department under this less than respected boss' tutelage. I worked in this organization for seven years, but always trying to scratch out acceptance clouded over because of an inglorious past. What had been expected of me prior to my first day of work and what the reality of the expectations became never meshed. I was forever at odds with the management of the organization. I vowed never to let such misunderstanding happen again.

An artist friend who trained as an art conservator works for a major American museum. Professionals in this field protect, reclaim, and repair all types of art and antiquities. Therefore, all the laboratory members so employed are expected to be professionals in their chosen specific field of art conservation whether it is painting, photography, paper and parchment, sculpture, etc. While some assignments might be given to a new conservator by the manager of the laboratory, all conservators are expected to be somewhat independent and capable of initiating projects immediately upon employment. They need to show willingness to undertake anything asked of them and they need to use their training and skill to create and enhance their own position.

The most difficult learning process in this and any other technical or skilled profession within such a large institution is adapting to entrenched processes and conditions. Newly-hired professionals must learn where to go and who to ask for any assistance that might be needed in the fulfillment of their specific project. Because each conservator is a professional with recognized skill, the institution's culture will expect each of them to find their way around and gather what information is needed using their own radar. The culture of such a large and multi-layered institution requires each conservator to fully establish his or her own credentials as a professional among other professionals. Once established, they can more easily maneuver through this long established and sometimes threatening culture. There are some advantages of having technical, artistic, or mechanical skills. The job expectations associated with physical elements can be seen, touched and felt. A professional conservator will know what scientific and technical procedures must be called upon to conserve a work of art. Contrast this with dealing only with the often hidden agendas of human ambitions and emotions in an office climate, and you have an entirely different kettle of fish. Keep that in mind as you prepare for a career. Is it technical, artistic, mechanical, or clerical and theoretical?

There are three *essentials* to unraveling job expectations as you initiate new employment. These essentials apply no matter what level of position you will be occupying from trainee up to and including CEO. These are:

• Have the essential expectations of your new position given to you in writing before you sign on the dotted line. This is especially critical if you have been hired through a third party—employment agency, recruiting service, or some agency assigned to fill your position. It's well known that some employment firms earn their fees based on a volume of business, with perhaps not enough thought being given toward the correct match between new employee and ultimate employer. Getting anything written from an employment service of any value may be difficult, but it will help make the difference toward your early success on the job. It will be more likely that a potential employer, rather than the employment service, would be willing, and perhaps welcome, the chance to spell out the expectations. Perhaps the employer has never put expectations to paper for anyone prior to your asking, so it will be good exercise for both employer and potential employee. Also, the potential employer will undoubtedly have greater respect for you as you put this request on the table. And it doesn't need to be a big deal. It's not that you're planning to sue the employer if the expectations have a different twist than the written page you received during the interviews. *Anytime you have a written document regarding any part of your job, you'll be in a stronger position to survive, should disagreements, misunderstandings, or controversy arise later on.*

• Insist on seeing a job description during the interview process. This document will differ from seeing the job expectations discussed in number one, above. The job description will be a road map of the details to help you fulfill the expectations. You should see this document before you decide whether or not the position is for you. There may be details you can't master or that you can't support. Job descriptions, if properly drafted, will lay out the relationship between this position and others within the organization. Remember, however, that job descriptions are living documents, subject to revision almost daily as new conditions arise and as new relationships are created within the organization. This will be *your* job description, so you need to keep it close at all times and, more importantly, you need to modify it as conditions change. Do not, *repeat, do not* let others control your job description. The more meaningful the job description, the more relevant is the job itself. As time goes on and your position gains more responsibility and relevance within the organization, the written job description will go a long way toward your getting higher pay and greater chances for promotions.

• If you are replacing a former person in this position, find out what happened to him/her and why that person is not still filling the chair. Fired? Promoted? Asked for a transfer to another department? Left voluntarily for different job in another organization? For any of these reasons, you need to gather additional intelligence to fully understand why this particular job is available. For example, if the person was fired, you need to know why. Was it because they couldn't relate well with the boss? Was it because they couldn't keep up with the expectations of the job? Was it because they caused dissension among the other staff members? Full knowledge of this information should give you a much better chance of survival if you take over the position. Of course, you may have difficulty getting as much information as you would like about the firing, but whatever you learn will be of help to you.

If, on the other hand the person holding the position couldn't keep up with the expectations of the job, you will have a much easier track as you move into the job. You should be able to learn where the problems developed and what expectations were unmet. With this information you can more easily establish your credentials by working very carefully to meet the expectations that were overlooked by the previous person on the job. Your boss will say, "Oh, that's great. You're doing a fine job. Sam (previous employee) never could master that part of our operations. Keep it up!" According to your boss, you are deftly handling the expected work of the terminated employee. But in addition to this work, you have other work not related to the missed expectations of the guy you replaced. If you're handling the balls dropped by your predecessor as well as doing all the work for which you were hired, you're in clover. You're doing your job, part of another's job, and saving the company money at the same time. This should look good at bonus time.

If your predecessor caused trouble and created dissension in the group, replacing a trouble maker should be a no-brainer for you. You yourself will never cause trouble, no matter what the temptation or what the conditions are that might encourage trouble-making. It just won't happen!

I once knew a situation where a woman had been employed to be the secretary for the Director of a non-profit institution. In addition to her secretarial duties, she was to assist with public relations and media connections. The first step she took on the job was to build a wall and moat around the Director. She took all calls, intercepted all mail, and would not let anyone see or speak with him without passing through her guard house. In this case she went substantially past the expectations of her job and totally annoyed the entire staff of the institution. It turned out that she was riddled with insecurities herself, was an unreformed alcoholic, and eventually had to be terminated by the very person she was working for and protecting. This is another item to be aware of. *Do not aggressively seek to outdo the expectations of your job as you know them to be.* You don't want to build animosity among your associates by trying to beat the system and outdo everyone else as you settle into a new position. This kind of action will often lead to a quick downfall.

In sales it might be another matter. If you commence to break sales records as a new recruit or even as a seasoned veteran recently hired from elsewhere, most other idiosyncrasies you might bring along with you will usually be overlooked. The other sales people and the sales support people might resent you, be jealous of you, and generally dislike you, but sales results mean a great deal to upper management, and after all, that group is paying you. So go for it!

LESSON III: When you commence any job, it is essential to know specifically what will be expected of you and to assure yourself that you can meet those expectations. Even more important, be in complete agreement with the person for whom you will be working so that you both understand and agree upon your job expectations.

CHAPTER FOUR

SURPRISES

Here's where the going gets rough. Often I would be driving between Pasadena, California and West Los Angeles by taking the usual expressway route of the Pasadena Freeway, then merging with Interstate 10 in downtown Los Angeles, and eventually onto the infamous "405." Late one afternoon as I approached the intersection of I-10 and I-405, traffic was backed up in a well-known L.A. congealed mess. Not prepared or familiar with this, it was a major SURPRISE. What to do now? I was in a hurry to return to my hotel in Century City to have dinner with another client. I suppose I shouldn't have been surprised by a Los Angeles traffic tie-up, but being only an occasional visitor to that part of the U. S., I hadn't figured out how the natives stay sane under such conditions. On another occasion I took the same route, and while conditions were less congested, there still were delays.

When unpleasant surprises arise, we need to learn how to survive under unexpected, and often, stressful conditions. There are many ways to attempt survival when blind-sided on the job, but here's what I did on the next drive from Pasadena to West L. A. I looked at the map! I discovered that by exiting I-10 at La Cienega Boulevard, I could take that main street, with all its intersections and stop lights, and maneuver my way to the hotel with relative ease. Even with stop and go traffic, I wasn't sitting stock still on a freeway, inhaling everyone's exhaust fumes, perspiring into my suit, and being late for the next appointment. To avoid the SURPRISE, I used a road map.

In our work lives we all need a road map or two. Here's another highway example for the East coast. Driving south on the New Jersey Turnpike, another infamous highway of misery, you might be surprised to hear on the car radio and see on the occasional overhead traffic warning sign that there is "congestion ahead". Rather than being SURPRISED by the fearsome warning signs, you plan ahead and take an exit where you know traffic will be moderate. Take an alternate route (US 130, US 1, or even I-295) if planning to leave the turnpike at exits 8 or 7 or lower. You've read the road map and you've learned how to avoid SURPRISES.

These simple examples of highway surprises and the means to avoid them can easily translate into employment situations. There will always be surprises confronting you in most any job. That's a guarantee. Therefore, you need to expect them. Don't let them alarm you, but plan a road map to assist you in making the appropriate detour around the surprises.

Moving off the highways and into the office environment, here's an example of a major surprise that shook all of us within a large insurance brokerage firm some years back. We had a rather tight department of about 40 individuals, all operating generally in unison, meeting our overall budget requirements, and not suffering undue pressure to change our direction. Suddenly! SURPRISE, SURPRISE! We were abruptly and without warning placed under the management of new executives imported from the Canadian division of the company. Their express purpose was to shake up our organization, create more new business results, and try to fashion our U.S. operations into a mirror image of their business model in Canada. People were interviewed, job descriptions were revised, termination papers were threatened, and overall morale dropped precipitously. I was particularly under the gun because I had been employed to create new business in a line not yet explored. My efforts, while eager, had produced meager results. I was faced with the dilemma of following the path I had been on and risking serious consequences or trying to develop a relationship with the new Canadian management to learn what, if anything, they could teach me. It seems that the team in Canada working on projects similar to mine was having acceptable success. But in reviewing my activities and product offerings to the American market, the situation, products, and marketing techniques used in Canada were substantially different than those that would succeed in the U.S. I knew almost immediately that the Canadian practices would not work in the U. S. In spite of my reservations, my new Canadian managers would not hear of my doing anything other than what had been successful in Canada. So what to do? How would I cope with this surprising and threatening development? I knew my job was on the line and that my days would have been numbered unless I produced results recommended by the boys from north of the border.

I decided on two routes on my road map. I did have a significant, very large, and prestigious local prospect that I had been quietly and diligently wooing for some time. I needed to continue to develop the possibilities with this local prospect and, at the same time, attempt to create a trusting relationship with the new management. The first route was to stall for time with the Canadians, by feigning real interest in their style of doing business. This required my attempting to cultivate some trust and friendship with their lead man, Lud. Lud drank large quantities of beer, so much of the time spent with him was in after-hours bar room discussions, which were mostly monologues on how we, in the U.S., should be doing business. The second route on my road map during regular business hours was to strengthen my relationship with this large, very important, prospective client to the point where the prospect might, in fact, become a client. One evening I would be out drinking beer with Lud, the Canadian, and getting an earful of unsolicited advice, then the next day there would be a lunch or meeting with the prospect. This heavy (and rather unhealthful) schedule continued until one fateful day, the coveted prospect gave the nod and moved from being a prospect to becoming a client. That quieted down much of the exhortations from Canada and assured my tenure for many years to come.

The strategy used in the face of this Canadian import surprise was a two route road map: first, becoming acquainted with the new and scorned management, spending some extra time socializing with them, listening, and appearing to be interested and understanding of their practices; and second, continuing to work on new business possibilities that I hoped would come my way. There was some stalling going on here, but this two route road map worked well for me.

Here are rules to help you deal with surprises:

• Expect that surprises will happen in any job and don't be surprised when you are surprised.
• Attempt to learn the nature of the surprises and how they may affect you, your performance, and the perception of the work you are attempting to accomplish.
• Make an honest effort to accommodate the conditions created by the surprises; that is, find a road map to help guide you through the orange cones or the detour signs.
• If your place of employment uses surprise technique often as a tool of management, I recommend that you consider new employment. Management by surprise is a cowardly way to run an operation and it definitely will not enhance the career of the diligent, hard working souls who live in the shadow of regular, but unexpected, surprises.

In any organization, there is always the risk of surprises being thrust upon you by unavoidable circumstances. These could include a sharp decline in revenue or market conditions; work interruptions caused by weather, fire, someone's death, your own illness or that of someone vital to a work process; or the sale or merger of the operation through which you are employed. Under these conditions, you will be caught up in the sudden changes along with everyone else in your community of work. This is where unity needs to prevail in order for the entire group to survive.

At the first underground bombing of the World Trade Center (WTC) in New York City in 1993, my office was one block south of the Trade Center and my apartment was in Battery Park City, across the highway from the WTC. Obviously, this was a tragic, sudden, unexpected, and extremely disruptive event for those who worked there. While not defined as a full act of war like the 2001 attack on the WTC, the 1993 attack was nevertheless a dastardly and well-coordinated feat of terrorism. This type of outrageous surprise won't be felt by most of us, but what impressed me after the attack was the unity of both the WTC tenants and others in the neighborhood. While the Trade Center buildings were closed to all tenants for some days, the management allowed people in for brief visits to remove vital work papers, etc. The entire Battery Park City (BPC) community helped with temporary facilities so jobs wouldn't be lost and vital work could be accomplished. We would see employees with wheel barrows, landscaping carts, and other hand vehicles trekking papers across the highway to buildings in Battery Park City where temporary quarters were established so work wouldn't be completely interrupted. People in BPC opened their apartments for use by displaced Trade Center personnel. Restaurants provided special meals late at night for those who worked on an unusual schedule. All in all there was cooperation and unity—elements that are essential for those caught in a major surprise like the WTC bombing or in destructive natural disasters such as hurricanes or extensive flooding.

In another position of my employment history, the CEO of the firm had been a kindly, much admired individual who had held his post for many years. Suddenly, he became seriously ill, entered the hospital, and died. SURPRISE! Not only had the corporate leader died, but the employees all felt the loss of a mentor and friend whom they admired and trusted. Not fully trusting of the newly self-appointed replacement leader, the staff nevertheless collected their talents, directed their efforts diligently, and created enough unity to assure the success and future growth of the organization without the leadership of the trusted and admired former CEO.

In any organization, no matter what its mission or its size, there will always be differences of opinions and sometimes even conflicts toward what steps to take to foster growth and success. That certainly was the case within the firm mentioned above. The firm was small enough that most individuals knew each other either by name or reputation. True, there were certain jealousies, areas of misunderstanding, even mistrust, and seeds of gossip within the fiber of the organization. Nevertheless, with the surprising and sudden death of a respected leader and the appointment of a replacement, unity prevailed. As the new leader took hold of the reins, the company prospered, somewhat changed direction, and proved that the new found unity was a strong force for survival. There could be countless examples of how unity has prevailed in the face of unwelcome surprises, but unity will be the surest and strongest glue to hold a family or an organization together in the face of unexpected or potentially disastrous surprises.

LESSON IV: Surprises will befall you in all parts of your life, whether it is within your employment or in your personal or family lives. With any surprise you must develop a road map to lead you through the unexpected and onto a balanced path toward the future. When surprises wield their sudden attack on any group, those in the group must develop immediate unity and strive together to create positive results from negative circumstances.

CHAPTER FIVE

CREATING ALLIANCES

In almost every employment situation, alliances can make or break successful time on the job. No other chapter in this book will be any more helpful than this one, so read it carefully and be determined that you will follow all the important suggestions as you watch closely how some of the interviewees have created alliances in order to survive. Here's an interesting first example:

A young lawyer accepted a position directly from law school in the Human Relations Department of a neighboring county government. In case you aren't aware, county governments have major control over the affairs of all the citizens. Counties determine what land will be developed, by whom, and the extent of any proposed development. In some states, county highway departments build and maintain the vast majority of roads within the county limits. County health departments give immunity shots to people of all ages, care for indigent pregnant women, and promote good health with lectures and demonstrations to the county school children. All land records back into the early history of the county are maintained in the county archives. In the more progressive counties, departments have been established to monitor and foster human relations among the citizens.

This particular county had a strong record in human relations and had been a leader within its state providing creative legislation and services to citizens suffering unfairly from one type of discrimination or another. In a staffing change, the County Manager had replaced a well-loved and effective middle line supervisor, with a new supervisor who, as described by a staff person, was tyrannical, dictatorial, and Machiavellian! Quite an indictment for a person employed to help provide equality, comfort, and opportunity for many who were denied those qualities of life.

There was no way any staffer could deal one on one with this supervisor. She had no ethics. She would deliberately lie to protect herself and would do nothing to protect the necks of her staff.

This brought an urgent need for unity among the entire staff supervised by this malevolent individual. So what did the staffers do effectively? First and foremost, they formed an unofficial, but quietly understood, alliance and at the same time they all agreed, as much as possible, to avoid contact with their mean and unsupportive supervisor. One might assume that ignoring your boss would be highly risky. Well, in this case, the boss was so devious that she actually appreciated being ignored so she could manage in her own mysterious way! They avoided sending documents or ideas through her for approval. When they could, without fear of discovery, they went over her head to more senior managers when an advocate was necessary. Several of these staffers were assigned outside the county government as liaisons with volunteer committees and commissions. So they expanded their alliance to include willing persons from these volunteer groups to be their advocates when such was necessary. The alliance had measurable effect on the working conditions of all the staffers, primarily because the supervisor pretty much ignored them and this allowed them to perform their own work quite effectively, even under these adverse conditions. This informal alliance had a telling effect on job performance and awakened the County Manager to the degree that this supervisor was placed under some investigation by senior county management regarding her leadership skill. Terminating a county employee is tricky business, so any investigation of an employee's performance must produce undeniable evidence of unsatisfactory behavior before the axe may be applied. No matter, however, what happened to the investigation of the supervisor, the staff alliance was a natural for protection from the wiles and unscrupulous ways of their supervisor. Eventually, after the county's tedious investigation was completed, the supervisor herself was given a new position of equal rank, but without any human management responsibility.

A recent *Knight Ridder* syndicated newspaper column by Marshall Loeb said bad bosses abound during times when more people are looking for jobs that do not exist. Bad bosses will work to get rid of staffers who are smarter or more efficient than the boss him/herself. And bad bosses do not go away. People with bad bosses must learn how to manage the situation and learn how to manage the boss. Loeb says, "Share your experiences and find out if other employees have found better ways to cope. Often it pays for you and several colleagues to approach the boss and tell him/her your grievances. He or she will find it hard to dispute or discipline all of you." This advice of Loeb's means to create alliances to help overcome the unbearable relationships with bad bosses. More about bosses later in this chapter.

Another value in creating alliances is to provide a ready path for moving ahead in the company or organization by which you are employed. A friend of mine worked in a middle management position in a large life insurance company. He was known in the community as a skilled performer who knew the intricacies of his products and also worked well with his office associates. A job offer came along from a major insurance brokerage firm that had a huge clientele of business customers and high income business owners and executives with needs for large life insurance policies. My friend said "no" and stayed where he was. Sometime later, however, the manager of the department where he would have worked in the brokerage house called again and offered a sweet alliance. Saying he was planning to retire in a few short years, if my friend joined him now, he would then be groomed to replace the manager. This was an alliance that was formed even before the job change took place, but it assured my friend that a management position awaited him at some future time. So my friend accepted the position and patiently awaited his ally's retirement so he could move into the vacancy. This situation proves without a doubt that alliances can be created to markedly enhance the careers of individuals.

My friend came into his management position by an alliance created while he was still outside the company. Inside your own work unit, it's not likely that you can build alliances to assist you in your own efforts to be promoted. Most employees aren't keen on helping a peer obtain a promotion, particularly if there is competition among equals for the next promotion. Within the organization, the alliance might well be with a supervisor or senior officer of the firm. This happened where I once was employed. A young man named Matt was hired. He had good credentials, coming from another respected firm. Immediately after starting on the job, he began to develop contacts and business alliances with several senior officers. He sought their advice. He introduced them to impressive prospective customers. He showed a wide knowledge of the company's products and services. This, of course, caused the people at his level to look at him with some suspicion and jealousy. Well, it didn't matter to Matt what his fellow workers felt or said. The new alliances he had created gradually took hold like trees burying their roots deeper in the soil, and before long he had hopped over several of his peers and obtained a strong leadership role in the organization. If you are using an alliance to improve your lot in the organization, you must be fully skilled to manage the new work you hope to obtain. If you fail to fulfill your new position skillfully, those in your alliance who might have assisted your climb will, to say the least, be disappointed, and they will most likely be the first to terminate the alliance unilaterally. Also, you must build the alliance in such a way your peers won't use target practice on you to sabotage your best efforts for moving ahead.

A young woman I interviewed began her consulting career with a company known at that time as Anderson Consulting—the management consulting arm of the big auditing and accounting firm, Arthur Anderson. Anderson Consulting spun themselves away from Arthur Anderson and chose a new name—Accenture. Arthur Anderson, also later, came under withering and destructive fire for condoning certain financial arrangements made by a major client, Enron, and both Enron and Arthur Anderson all but disappeared from the corporate road maps. My friend, Gerial, joined Anderson along with many other young college and business school graduates. For many, the work assignments given to new associates were the least attractive, the most tedious, boring, and often required weeks and weeks of hotel living in strange cities or countries. Early on, Gerial was fortunate in receiving an assignment with a partner who was a pleasure to work with and who appreciated her ability and praised her results. It was now time for Gerial to strike an alliance with this partner. They arranged it so she would be his junior consultant on all of his assignments. For her, this meant interesting assignments, a supportive partner, and much better learning opportunities rather than the usual routine of being chosen from "the line-up" like most newcomers to Anderson.

Before you set about creating alliances, it is essential that you know the need for the alliance and, more important, that you fully trust the motives of those with whom you pursue the alliance. On a grand international scale, during World War II, which was fought from 1939-1945, and after the U. S. joined the war in 1941 following the Japanese attack on Pearl Harbor, Hawaii, the U. S. was allied with Great Britain, France, China, and later on during the war, with an amalgam of Eastern European and Asian nations that called themselves the Soviet Union. The alliances with Britain and France remain to this day, but very shortly after the war ended, relations with the Soviet Union deteriorated rapidly to the point that an ally quickly became an adversary. There were threats of nuclear destruction from both sides. Military build-ups on each side hopefully served as a deterrent to a nuclear holocaust. And the same fear and distrust developed between the U.S. and China. With great military forces growling at each other, what had been a war-winning alliance turned into a peace threatening stand-off. So the critical point for anyone forming an alliance for success is to fully understand the motives of your allies in order to be completely assured that the ultimate objectives of all parties in the alliance are compatible. With a "think alike" and "do alike" alliance, you will work together and withstand any predators that might wish to fracture the team.

Here is a set of rules you must use in establishing an alliance within your job situation:

• Be certain that any person with whom you might become allied is firmly established in their job. If they are more insecure than you, their motives will differ from yours. If their position suffers some instability, avoid them.

• Before you establish this alliance associated with any specific job detail or issue you wish to tackle, create a trusting and open friendship connected to topics other than job related issues. Learn something about your target—interests, family, history, etc. Make the target feel comfortable with you and start to develop trust with each other. Remember, in Chapter One, the advice was to allow yourself to become vulnerable. Careful vulnerability will assure you trust and friendship from those worthy of your trust and friendship. If your vulnerability is taken advantage of and misused, make no further efforts to create this alliance.

• If you and your ally(ies) intend to make a case for specific action of any kind from your employer, be fully prepared. For any meeting, have prepared notes which you take into the meeting and refer to the notes during the meeting. And LOOK YOUR TARGET DIRECTLY IN THE EYES! You and your allies must be solid in your beliefs, prepared with the necessary facts or figures, and committed to stay with one another during any confrontation. You must support each other and not allow a split to develop among allies.

If in your employment situation things are going smoothly and you have no need for any confrontation with your boss or anyone else, you still will need allies in order to make your every day work more pleasant and enriching. Friends whom you trust provide a great deal of comfort and encouragement in any employment situation. A book entitled *Problem Bosses* was co-authored by Dr. Mardy Grothe and Dr. Peter Wylie, Facts on File Publications. They have an excellent presentation of the value of strong alliances, especially when confronting a boss and hoping for relief from specific problems. In their scenario, a group of employees banded together to confront their boss about his office behavior. The boss had a mercurial temper. He pouted. He could be very moody. He even resorted to violence occasionally—not against employees, but destructive behavior taken out against furniture and other physical objects.

In order to be able to confront the boss and hope for improved behavior, one employee assumed leadership of the effort. She carefully screened several employees in whom she could trust and together they planned a strategy of confrontation. The employees she chose all had different personality characteristics and because of these differences would strengthen the presentation to the boss. They all met several times, planning who would say what. They actually did some role playing. Then the team leader had the responsibility of making the appointment with the boss. She took the approach with him that she and her fellow employees intended to speak about ways to make his job more satisfying and less frustrating. During her efforts to set up the larger meeting, some sparks flew, but the boss finally acceded to the meeting and after careful rehearsal, the "confrontation" meeting was held. To everyone's surprise and relief, the boss was also fully prepared and made the meeting move swiftly and smoothly to a final and cooperative conclusion. The boss realized that his staff seriously desired to make his life less frustrating and more satisfying and the boss realized that his unacceptable behavior needed to change. It definitely was a carefully planned alliance of individuals who understood the problem and banded together toward a mutually satisfactory solution.

LESSON V: In any workplace, alliances are essential, whether just for friendship, or to promote and enhance the employment conditions.

You must be able to totally trust those with whom you make alliances. If trust can't be assured, there should be no alliance.

Your motives should be equally honorable; strong and trusting alliances provide rewards in employment far beyond the needs of the moment.

CHAPTER SIX

OBEY THE STOP SIGNS

This can be the most deceptive and sensitive aspect of any job in any organization. Most of the deception is caused by managers at any level from first line supervisors up to and including CEO's who attempt to paint a results picture more rosy than real. There are many ways to juggle numbers—some perfectly legal, but nevertheless, deceptive. Remember the corporate crashes of the early 21st century—Enron, Tyco, WorldCom, and several others? These large and apparently thriving organizations were spewing out quarterly numbers which looked quite good to security analysts as well as investors. In reality, however, financial officers within the firms, with the general concurrence of their outside auditors, were skewing financial results that, in fact, were ultimately proven to be untrue and eventually disastrous. Once these financial executives started on this downward slide to oblivion, they continued to skew the numbers, hoping that 1) they would not get caught, and 2) that conditions would develop within the companies to support the numbers they created.

In an extensive report in the June 23, 2003, issue of the *Wall Street Journal*, the situation was graphically explained how WorldCom executives sailed through the stop signs which sadly, led to prison terms for some. An accounting manager, Betty Vinson, known as a diligent and cooperative employee, was told to dip into a reserve account and take out $828 million to cover some huge pending losses. This by itself would have been an illegal transaction, and the stop signs began madly flashing. Unfortunately for Ms. Vinson, she and her associates did what they were told and sailed right through them.

As conditions continued to worsen at WorldCom, Scott Sullivan, Chief Financial Officer of the company, conjured up another creative, but illegal, solution to make the books look satisfactory for Wall Street analysts. He ordered the accountants, including Ms. Vinson, to improperly charge $771 million of operating expenses as capital expenses. When Ms. Vinson heard of this planned transfer, she was shocked, but dutifully ignored the stop sign and reluctantly did as she was asked. In WorldCom's flagrant case of fraud, several executives, including Ms. Vinson, were criminally convicted.

The WorldCom fraud and eventual bankruptcy clearly showed that no matter how one skews an organization's numbers, the truth will eventually surface. Honest numbers are protected by internal audits, external audits, product sales in the market place, and a host of checks and balances designed to produce honest and accurate numbers. There are ways, however, by using creative financial instruments and by transferring assets made to look like profits that a lengthy drama of deception can run for years!

Corporate executives can reward themselves handsomely—until the house of cards collapses under its own creatively dishonest weight. During the entire duration of this drama, warning lights will flash from yellow to red, but the people driving the runaway locomotive will continue to ignore the lights and the stop signs until it's much too late. Then all the accumulated wealth and the public adulation they have been receiving will turn into civil and criminal indictments and scorn. They then can be seen in newscasts or in the daily paper leaving the courthouse in handcuffs or holding their hands in front of their faces to avoid prying cameras. Usually, the perpetrators have been aware of the huge risks they have been undertaking while these financial scams were under way. Unfortunately for them, greed and short lived glory kept the train hurtling along the track, ignoring the red stop signs and into oblivion. It was fun while it lasted, but, oh, the pain of getting caught!

These big corporate deals make the headlines, attract the attention of the regulators, and give the talk show hosts plenty of meat for hours of punditry. On the day to day level most of us are familiar with however, there may also be stop signs we need to observe in order to keep our work site running smoothly and to assure our survival on the job.

Obeying the stop signs is not always about greed and public adulation, however. Keith, a young friend of mine, saved his career and swallowed a bitter defeat by obeying the stop signs. He worked in a highly-regarded and world-renown medical center as a patient advocate/social worker. His job included seeing that discharged patients were sent to the correct places—their homes, nursing homes, other medical centers, etc. He dealt with many organizations outside his own medical center, negotiating with insurance companies, arranging treatment or admission to other institutions, and following up on the welfare of many discharged patients.

In dealing with so many patients, he became aware that most of the Latino patients who came for treatment had no health insurance and very limited assets and incomes. That meant that his center was footing the bulk of the expense for whatever treatment was necessary. No patient was turned away. He did some careful research and calculated the many millions of dollars lost annually by the institution due to inadequate reimbursement for the treatment of these patients. He also discovered that there were additional resources available that would help subsidize this loss without having to diminish or compromise patient care. This meant that the center needed a strong and creative person to write the federal grant requests and to continue to interact with the local Latino community—which was growing every day. He took it upon himself to draw up the specifications for a new professional in the medical center to write these grant requests and to work within the local Latino community. He also worked diligently within the institution to position himself for the appointment when the job was approved by senior leadership.

Following usual protocol for a new position, he, among others, applied for the position and the job was actually promised him by a hospital administrator. The job would entail some interacting with these Latinos (he spoke fluent Spanish), but additionally he would be cultivating other resources and strategies to reduce these financial losses, making the medical center basically whole for the treatment and care being given these immigrants—many of whom were working in the area without proper immigration credentials.

Of course, the medical center needed to advertise internally to fill this position even though this man had been promised it. Well, you can surmise what happened. The job went to another employee—a Latino woman who appeared to be a more politically correct candidate to fill this spot. My friend was livid and sorely disappointed with this announcement. He had personally and individually seen the need and convinced the medical center's administration of the value of this position from both a financial and public relations standpoint. And he didn't get the job!

Where do the stop signs figure in this unfortunate event? I'll tell you. With the rug pulled completely out from under him after he had been promised the job, he sought retribution against the institution and to see that justice was served. A law suit seemed the best possibility, so he sought the advice of an attorney. These discussions told him that a suit would only give him limited financial reward, but, more to the point, his career within the institution would be jeopardized and his reputation as a sore loser and a malcontent could easily prevent him from finding satisfactory employment again in the community where he lived and hoped to remain. These were the stop signs: 1) little financial reward for a big legal effort; 2) a severely tarnished reputation; 3) possible future employment problems in his chosen occupation. So he went to the senior administration of the medical center and told them that he had considered taking legal action, but he had accepted the overall decision of the institution and decided that he wouldn't pursue the issue any further. Management breathed a collective sigh of relief, but my friend did say he hoped justice would be done. Lo and behold, shortly after that, justice was served as the administrator who had promised him the position in the first place received notice of termination.

The stop signs had become very apparent to my friend. By obeying them he retained his present position, saved unnecessary notoriety and expense, and continued to work within the institution where he had built a solid reputation as well as the respect of the medical staff who worked with him.

Many, however, do not obey the stop signs and thus find themselves facing negative results for themselves or others for whom they might be responsible. Here's a story of a small group of sales and service people who went through the stop signs and suffered severe injuries. These folks were a unit of men and one support person (female) assigned to sell group insurance to small businesses and to provide client service to these same small businesses. One of the men was able to find leads from sources he developed and had reasonable success selling new customers. The other two men performed their service effectively—too effectively, however, and spent little time developing new business. Weekly activity reports were required and week after week, there were blank lines on the pages where new business sales figures should have appeared. Senior management regularly questioned the line supervisor as to these negative results. There were plenty of excuses, but still no results. In other words, the stop signs, or in this case, the warning signs, were flashing—"Do something! Show us some results!"

With the lights flashing right in front of these non-producers they continued to ignore the messages. Excuses began to wear thin, and, one day the senior management lowered the boom and said, "fire the two non-producers as well as the woman support person." In this situation the flashing signs were telling these non-producers to "GO—SHOW SOME RESULTS." Ignoring the flashing signs meant total unemployment for three persons, all three of whom had reasonable longevity working for the organization. Ignoring the stop signs will eventually bring on the inevitable. They cannot be ignored.

In another sad situation, a married man working for a large organization began surreptitiously dating a recently divorced secretary. Have you heard this before? It does, as you might expect, happen with predictable regularity. This large organization happened to have as a major client a large religious denomination. Therefore, many of the organization's employees were devoted members of this same denomination. The person who supervised these illicit lovers knew of the affair and threw up several stop signs, but affairs like this one, with new found intimacy, are difficult to throttle back. In this case, the affair continued until an anonymous letter was written to senior management by a shocked employee who spilled the beans. The word came down: "fire them both." That's what happened. They both were quickly shown the door after they had ignored the stop signs and continued their formerly secret liaison. You'll read more about job-related sex in the next chapter, but this scenario testifies how not obeying the stop signs led to standing in the line at the unemployment insurance office, particularly after unapproved sex had entered the mix.

A very typical scenario of ignoring stop signs goes something like this.

• A company, group, department, or whatever has an objective to meet a certain growth level during a certain period of time.
• Revenue results are falling somewhat behind plan and management needs to take action to meet the plan.
• Sales orders are coming in, but orders do not translate into revenue until delivery has been made and the product or service has been paid for.
• Management decides to record unpaid orders into revenue with the full expectation that the actual revenue will follow.

• In a sudden economic downturn, some orders falter, however, and the spread between actual orders and paid revenue widens. Everyone up and down the line knows what is happening, but they all look aside, ignoring the stop signs that tell them that this gap between orders and paid revenue will not only widen, but will become more obvious and therefore difficult to overcome.

• Company internal auditors make a routine check of department accounting procedures and discover this revenue imbalance. Department management is forced to admit their misallocation of the numbers, and agrees to balance the orders against actual revenue.

• Once the auditors leave, management realizes that rather than fudging phantom revenue, major expense cuts would be a cleaner way to meet the budget numbers.

• Immediate expense reductions are now initiated. These reductions include termination of several staff persons, clamping down on travel and entertainment costs, reducing year end bonuses, and postponing expense charges until a later accounting period. Once again, by postponing expense charges, the numbers are being skewed and stop signs will be flashing. As with any such delay of current expenses, the piper will eventually be paid, if not in the next accounting period, but soon thereafter. In this example, the immediate problem had been fixed, and only with minor fallout.

Two stop signs were ignored: 1) do not advance revenue against future actual payment, and 2) do not postpone current expense charges into a future accounting period.

The department leadership, having been discovered by the auditors, had the opportunity to clear the decks and change direction by reporting revenue correctly. Nevertheless, by ignoring the stop signs until that day of discovery, reputations, employment for some, and respect were lost. Then by turning right around and postponing expense charges until a later time, the leadership continued to run the risk of discovery and thus were still ignoring the stop signs. Temptations to turn the head and ignore obvious stop signs sometimes are overwhelming. Rarely can one zoom right through the stop signs without a collision. Frequently the collision will be fatal!

LESSON VI: Stop signs are usually obvious and don't sneak up on individuals. There are usually enough warnings so that the stop signs can't be ignored.

When more than one person is aware of the stop signs, they need to act in unison to see that the signs are obeyed and to assure survival.

Often pointing out the stop signs makes one a "whistle blower." This designation can often lead to unpleasant consequences. The "whistle blower" needs to be prepared to run for cover. This often means changing jobs to avoid harassment and abuse.

CHAPTER SEVEN

A CAULDRON OF SEX

"Cauldron - a kettle or boiler," according to *Webster's Collegiate Dictionary, 10th Edition.* It's the boiler part of this brief definition that I want to focus upon in this chapter. Boiling means hot. Too much heat can burn. Burning brings pain. Excessive pain can lead to permanent disabling and the inability to function effectively, or not at all. That is what sex can do with a person's job survival and, ultimately, to the effectiveness of a unit, department, or even a complete organization.

This chapter will not be a moral treatise or sermon about sin or the evils of unacceptable sexual activity between consenting adults. This chapter will vividly point out the unavoidable difficulties that will befall individuals and impair their survival possibilities as they participate in unacceptable sexual involvement within a work environment. Off-the-job sexual activity should be private, personal, and mostly of no consequence to employers, unless off-the-job activity spills over onto the workplace. But on-the-job is another matter. Let me explain.

In the previous chapter I mentioned the ultimate employment termination of two individuals who developed a heterosexual relationship while working on my staff. The man was heading to a divorce and the woman had been divorced. When their secret romance became known and the word came from above to terminate them, they were rather deep into the relationship. They each left immediately, leaving two holes in the department. The marked couple eventually married and for all I know, lived together happily. But their transgression made life more complex for those who needed to take over their work assignments. More significantly, however, the folks remaining in the unit thereafter were looked on with a certain degree of suspicion. "How could they have let this affair develop? Who else in the department might be doing the same thing?" Personally, I felt the hot breath of suspicion on my management style and I eventually was forced to move on. In other words, the two love birds did not survive in this particular workplace and certain others with whom they were associated also were burned, felt the pain from their affair, and eventually also failed to survive.

In the early years of my career I was employed in sequence in similar positions by two large financial institutions. My first job was in a headquarters environment where men and women of all ages worked together and lived in middle sized urban and suburban areas in Connecticut. Employees and their families became well acquainted, interacted socially, and maintained ongoing cordial relationships, many even into their retirement. This was during the time when men had most of the better jobs, but still, there were many well educated, dedicated, career-oriented women working right along with the men. The culture, fortunately, was quite wholesome as it related to male/female relationships. Even at office holiday events, where only employees were in attendance, there seemed to be mutual gender respect and almost no action took place that could have caused even a slightly raised eyebrow. Perhaps I was naïve in those early days of my career, but even later when I occasionally met and reminisced with former fellow employees and spouses, never was there a mention of unacceptable sexual activity among our former associates. I remembered fondly both the actual work activities among my fellow employees as well as the friendly social times together with employees, spouses, and our children. In the American society, reference is frequently made, especially from the political stump, about "family values." What these values are is usually left undefined. Some office holders and candidates have more or less built an entire campaign on their waving the "family values" flag. No matter how many empty references to "family values" fill the air, it is most likely that many of us would define these values as people bound together by trust, high ethical and moral standards, and respect for one's associates. My first work opportunity described in the above paragraph is a clear example of how honest-to-goodness "family values" fostered healthy and respectful relations among all persons, without fear or anxiety of any sexual exploitation.

With a change in locations and companies, a dramatically different script was written! The second job (same type of work in the same industry) was in New York City where there was next to no personal interaction among employees after 5:00 p.m. They all rushed for their public transportation to other parts of the city or to the suburbs. Interrelations among employees and their respective families were basically non-existent. The company was smaller than the first, but sold the same products and services, albeit through different marketing techniques. But what each of these companies sold or through what marketing techniques made little difference. The major difference between the companies was the interpersonal relationships among employees—particularly between some of the men with several of the women. While I said above that there was almost no personal interaction among employees, what there was, however, often proved to be socially unacceptable.

One story, possibly apocryphal, had to do with the CEO himself who, during a company holiday party in a local hotel, was discovered during the event (by whom was never revealed) naked in bed with an equally naked secretary—his secretary, alas! The fact that this story even was related over the years gives some cause for suspicion, due to the fact that the source of the person discovering this tawdry event never seemed to be revealed. Nevertheless, the story itself can be the beginning of several "in bed" relationships that seemed to be a part of the corporate culture of that company.

One single, well respected professional female staffer came up to me one day and said, "The trouble with most of you men is that you go home to the suburbs every night to your wives when you could be enjoying the company of interesting women in the city." This was an open invitation that I, fortunately, was able to acknowledge with a smile but with a "no thanks," as I went home to my wife. Another story was related to me by an associate who was chatting with a young woman in the company's media relations department and when he suggested that the two of them should get together, she said, "you name the time and the place." Well, he named the time and the place where they met several times over until she left the company for another job. He never heard from her or saw her again. This encounter did nothing to hurt my associate's survival problem, but it is an example of the generally free sexual climate within that organization.

One of the newly hired sales persons under my supervision was assigned to open and manage a company office in Philadelphia. He was married, with several small children, and lived in a New York City suburb. While in Philadelphia, he stayed in a one room furnished apartment, but always came home to his family on the weekends. Unfortunately for his short career with this firm, he became actively involved with a sexually charged (as he described her) single woman in Philadelphia, who not only took time from his work performance, but somehow infected his marriage to the point that his wife knew what was happening and caused a righteous uproar. That ended his job with the firm in Philadelphia or anywhere else. He came back to New York and hoped to save his troubled marriage. While his sexual activity was not with a fellow employee, his off-the-job indulgence was just as devastating and his survival was short lived. This is a vivid example that has been repeated many times over. Many careers have been shattered by overindulgence in unacceptable sex.

A headline in a *Wall Street Journal* article of November 13, 2003, said, "Co-Workers Can Wreck a Marriage: At the office, divorce is contagious." The article, written by Sue Shellenbarger, reported on a seven-year study of 37,000 employees at 1,500 work places which provided empirical evidence that working with people of the opposite sex is hazardous to marriage. Ms. Shellenbarger goes on to say, "working with co-workers who are all of the opposite sex increases the divorce rate by a startling 70%, compared with an office filled with co-workers of the same sex."

Another quote in the same article was from David Poponoe of the National Marriage Project at Rutgers University who said that in the office, "it doesn't matter whether you're married or not. It's open season." Divorce cases in the office are contagious. According to this same source, a person is 43% more likely to get divorced if one-third of his or her co-workers are recently divorced people of the opposite sex than if none of the co-workers were recently divorced.

Another source reported in the same article was a 2002 study done by Janet Lever of California State University, Los Angeles. More than half of the married respondents to Dr. Lever's survey admitted that when a co-worker flirted with them for fun, they flirted back. Dr. Lever said, "What starts out as 'just fun' can escalate. And clearly, the marrieds are not out of the loop."

From time to time, relationships on the job do manage to blossom into long time romances and even successful marriages with or without children. One young couple I know both worked for a major financial institution and became acquainted while working in the same department. A friendship developed into a romance which had both of them terrified should the word get out that they were into heavy dating. As luck would have it, the male of the couple was suddenly transferred to a subsidiary organization half way across the continent, so their fear of discovery was muted by the distance between them. Even while separated, the courting continued at a distance until they decided to "go public" with their romance and announced their engagement. Shortening this love story so as not to bore you with acceptable domesticity, the two did marry. The husband eventually took the entrepreneurial route and the wife stayed with the organization and became a member of the senior management team. I guess we could say "they lived happily ever after."

A similar romance that began "off limits" developed between a graduate school professor and his student in a highly respected state university. Making matters more risky for this potentially illicit couple, another professor at the same university had been dismissed because of unacceptable sex with one or more students. My friends, however, decided that their relationship was developing into deep feelings of love and respect. Their course of action was also to "go public" with university officials. This gave them the green light to continue the dating and shortly thereafter they became engaged and married. Correct intentions will bring satisfying, and even joyous rewards.

The expectations of unacceptable work site activity have reached the point where men and women working closely together often feed rumors even though the parties are fully innocent. For about two years in my final job as an employee of a large company and before I founded Hendrickson & Company, I traveled from time to time to participate in annual conventions sponsored by trade associations. Occasionally, accompanying me was an attractive, vivacious, recently divorced blonde employee who not only wooed the attendees and spouses toward the insurance offerings we were presenting, but was a knowledgeable and professional representative of our firm. To further feed the rumors, the two of us occasionally lunched together back in our home city and accompanied each other to industry functions. But rumors persisted and even after I had departed the firm, former associates approached me with winks and sly comments about my relationship with Rosemary. The point of this recital is to emphasize that as professional work becomes more intimate, rumors will emerge. The safest approach is to ignore the rumors and continue to work together as true professionals, enjoying each other as persons and respecting each other's individual personal lives.

Problems with sex aren't related only to intimate and unacceptable activities. From time to time a man will treat a woman or women with little respect and harass them verbally, physically, or through job discrimination. A strikingly discriminatory situation developed with a friend of mine—a brilliant and successful analyst in the investment business. She worked for a major Wall Street firm and specialized in analysis work with derivatives and other mysterious and delicate instruments in the investment world. She had (and still has) uncanny powers of intuition and was able to provide investment advice on these esoteric instruments that provided substantial profit for her firm.

Her work life was running smoothly until her manager hired a friend of his who had recently been terminated by a competing firm. It was both the friendship and the promises of outstanding performance results that prompted the hiring, not necessarily the previous work record of the new man. Settling into the job, he was quick to recognize that my female friend was producing circles around him and around many others in the firm. This not only surprised, but petrified the new man, and he realized that he would need to muscle in on some of her territory in order to meet his rosy production promises. That didn't work. The young woman built a veritable moat around herself and began producing at an even higher level. She left her new adversary in a trail of blue smoke and, while producing greater profits for the firm, also succeeded in making enough income for herself so that she became financially independent. This brought direct vocal and abusive reaction from the new man in town. His harassment was so vicious that she finally left the firm, hired an attorney, and brought an arbitration hearing against him for sexual harassment. This was one jealous man who used sexual harassment as a weapon to enhance his own survivorship. It didn't work. He had picked the wrong target.

In this case the woman survived the harassment, but because of it, did not want to survive any longer at the same firm. Being personally on a solid financial base, she left the firm and while the arbitration case was in the works, took her sweet time seeking replacement employment. Last I spoke with her, she was employed by a well-managed hedge fund—a type of investment company where her intuitive abilities were both respected and well rewarded.

A tragic case of sexual harassment occurred in a small insurance office on the west coast. The manager, a rather explosive individual, not only verbally abused a woman staffer, but he physically abused her. Within days, his job was pulled out from under him and he needed to scramble quickly in order to support his family of a wife and three young daughters. His survival with his employer ended sharply and he found himself working independently for the remainder of his career. The living conditions of his family sank to new low levels, at least temporarily, until he built his own practice. While this explosive bit of sexual harassment knocked him to his knees, he was able to overcome the serious setback and avoid such behavior during the years that followed. Sexual abuse as well as unacceptable sexual intimacy can quickly destroy careers and guarantee the end of job survival.

The power of activities related to sex in our lives start at early ages. Pre-teen boys and girls stay away from the other sex because they primarily prefer their own gender as they are learning about life in school and out. Teens sometimes jump into easy friendship with their sexual opposites. Other teens still hang around with their own sex and feel more comfortable that way. A few teens begin to explore intimate physical activity with the opposite sex which, as we all know, can lead to teen pregnancies, early transmission of sexually transmitted diseases, school drop outs, and early dependence on public assistance—primarily for young women.

In the next stage of human development into young adulthood and into the work place, sex can become a dominant factor in young lives. In many cases, men and women follow a traditional path and marry. Other young adults remain single, some for many years, and can be found to lead a celibate existence. Others who remain single explore both heterosexual and homosexual lives, some with multiple partners, others monogamous. The danger begins to slowly erupt like an awakening volcano when sexual activity interferes with life on the job. Whether the sexual activity is intimate between two consenting partners and, hopefully, away from the eyes of nosy co-workers, or whether it becomes annoyingly visible with outright discrimination and/or harassment, it signals major warning signs and usually generates both heat and pain.

LESSON VII: Enjoying sex with a loving partner is humanity's most blessed experience. Attempting sexual relations secretly with an associate at work can be a devastating experience. Enjoy your working relationships with both men and women in your work place and treat all persons with respect and courtesy. Be blind to sexual differences. As a manager, be an equal opportunity person and reward results based on performance only. Avoid prejudicial decision making, whether your actions relate to a homosexual or heterosexual person. At all costs, avoid any type of intimate, unacceptable relationship with any person in your workplace or even outside the workplace, if the relationship will diminish your on-the-job efficiency and interfere with your ultimate survival.

CHAPTER EIGHT

STAYING UNDER THE RADAR

Here is a story of the longest and most successful effort of anyone I have known, heard of, or even interviewed who managed to stay under the radar and survive for decades in a strong and healthy fashion. Not only did this one individual stay under the radar, but his entire small unit managed to remain out of sight while doing their jobs year after year, merger after merger.

Charlie had been a rising commercial lending officer in a large New York bank, when in the 1970s he was tapped to manage a specialty marketing program that was directed to sell a non-bank service to hundreds of smaller banks across the country. He was apprehensive about the potential of the new assignment, but it was something new and entirely different than lending money, so he jumped in head first, deciding to give it his all. This particular New York bank (Manufacturers Hanover, defined as a "money center" bank) was well known within the banking community for offering banking services and several other non-bank related services to these smaller, often rural banks, in every other state of the union. Charlie took over this program which had, more or less, been an orphan inside the bank. Several executives at Manufacturers Hanover gave it lip service, but made no effort to improve the marketing results. The program was so small and out of the way that no one had even measured the financial results as to whether or not it was profitable or a loser. Big businesses often have these niche operations, and usually when they get picked up by the radar, they are jettisoned. But Charlie had other ideas.

Starting out in this new position, Charlie had a staff of two others in addition to himself. He became a quick student of a business he knew nothing about—employee benefit plans that his bank was offering to these many small banks. He learned by developing strong and trusting relationships with outside employee benefit specialists—especially those who saw new marketing opportunities as Charlie revved up this previously moribund program. Slowly he began to add new services and products. He set up seminars among small banks in various states and began to develop relationships with bank CEO's all over the country. As the sales and revenue results grew, he added more staff until he had at least eight people working in his unit.

The bank itself began to refine its internal reporting results and suddenly Charlie's unit had numbers attached to it—small numbers, but at least the results finally could be measured against other sections of the bank. By and large, this particular program was small change compared to other services the money center bank sold around the country. In fact, it was so small and so unrelated to banking that there was active consideration toward wrapping it up and selling it to an outside vendor. After testing the waters and receiving bids from potential buyers, the decision was made that, even with its small size, the profit margins were acceptable, so the bank squelched the idea of selling it and decided to keep it around. In addition to the acceptable profit of the unit, the staff and services helped in the overall relationships with hundreds of small bank clients, and "relationships" are the backbone of successful banking.

More to the point, there were other departments of the bank marketing a variety of insurance services to the bank's corporate customers and these departments were lurking in the shadows, coveting Charlie and his tidy profit margins to add to their operations. Year after year, Charlie had the knack of dodging what might have been a fatal bullet from these other departments which would, in all likelihood, have reduced his management responsibility and impaired his personal paycheck. There were several things Charlie did consistently that assured the stability of his unit and kept it well under the radar, such as: 1) Charlie kept a tight rein on his small staff so that they remained loyal to him and more or less kept to themselves; 2) he developed a close tie to his various immediate supervisors, constantly reminding whomever was in charge at the moment of the superior job he and his staff were doing as their bottom line profits continued to swell; and 3) each of his many supervisors over the years were traditional bankers and knew little of the finer points of Charlie's products and services. He purposely kept them well in the dark about these details.

Closely adhering to these three management techniques kept him aboard exactly where he wanted to remain. His bosses changed regularly (he must have had at least ten during the 25 years I was acquainted with his operation) and through his careful maneuvering, he stayed right where he was—low down under the searching radar, producing acceptable financials, and keeping his bosses comfortably happy. Those of us on the outside would periodically shake our heads in wonderment as to his ability to chug along in one place while others around him were stressed out through mergers, layoffs, and other corporate turmoil. During his tenure, mergers of big New York banks were almost daily events. First, Manufacturers Trust merged with The Hanover Bank forming Manufacturers Hanover. Next Chemical Bank and Manufacturers Hanover merged, forming a new Chemical Bank. A few years later, a suffering Chase Manhattan Bank needed help and merged into Chemical while the name "Chase" became the chosen identity. Then along came the crusty and tradition bound J. P. Morgan Company, an organization and name that had symbolized wealth and power, but that had fallen on strained financial conditions, so it was blended into the new Chase and the whole shebang was christened "J. P. Morgan Chase." During all these mergers, while there often had been near slaughter around him, *he never was forced to downsize nor even give anyone from his staff an early retirement package.* Once he built his staff to eight, it became a permanent number, cast in cement.

The minute he retired the vultures swooped in and before many months had elapsed, his chosen replacement had been swallowed up by the much larger departments of the bank and conditions changed radically. The remaining staff, the customers, and the nature of the products and services this tight little band of loyalists had marketed and managed effectively for more than 25 years were totally disrupted. Without Charlie's protective instincts, the radar finally found its quarry and allowed the heavy guns to be trained on it.

I outlined in Chapter Six the story of the young man working at the medical center who had obeyed the stop signs and avoided a major confrontation after the disappointment of being by-passed for a position he had been promised. His institution, like many others, faced budget turmoil which forced lay-offs and early retirement packages. He could easily have been singled out for termination had the institution sensed that he was angry and unfulfilled by the career rejection he had faced. He carefully kept on with his job, working closely with the senior medical staff in his department, gaining their full confidence and keeping his head down throughout the entire medical center. Survival for him meant gaining the support of the medical staff he worked with. This was a highly-respected, vitally essential, and world-renowned medical unit of the institution. By working quietly and efficiently, staying close to his own base of operations and not on the lookout for promotion or other opportunities within the medical center, his survival was assured. As the radar beams circled the air above him, he was safely below their reach and secure in his position.

Staying under the radar is not always easy—in fact, it often takes some doing to be purposely avoided while others are moving up or out. My friend, Buck, worked for a major financial institution in New England and began his 40 year career in a unit serving the needs of the men in the remote offices (there were no women in those days doing sales work in these remote offices. Times do change, however. As this book is being written, this same type of work is shared equally between men and women).

As his career moved along, his activity branched out into providing specialized market research for these sales personnel in the remote offices. Buck was not professionally trained as a market research specialist, but his assignments filled several niches within the company at a much lower cost than that of retaining a professional market research organization to do the same job. The company chose not to build its own internal market research staff nor did they retain such firms on the outside. Buck was it for some time. Buck would visit these remote field offices from time to time, taking the loyalty temperature of the field personnel, returning to the home office, and writing voluminous reports with his findings. The irony of this job was that the home office management often knew the needs of the field—their product demands, the level of staff morale, and the activity of the competition. Even so, the home office management personnel read his reports with eagerness since Buck's reports presented a broad, system-wide synopsis of market and staff conditions.

The position that Buck built kept him well under the radar. Why? He was not programmed for higher management spots nor did he plan to transfer into the field offices and assume a salesman role where the financial rewards could have been substantial. He provided honest appraisals of the conditions he found around the country. He was a talented writer, so his reports read well and didn't bore the readers. He accepted assignments as they were meted out and totally stayed under the radar until he retired with a pension after 40 years of loyal service. In many firms I have analyzed, people like Buck, who aren't groomed for promotions into senior levels, are offered a one way exit. Buck had a talent that was appreciated by his superiors which allowed him to stay aboard the company he loved until retirement. And, because he played well in the role he chose, he has remained personally close to many of his associates, many of whom were several levels above him during his working years. There is a huge risk, however, by purposely trying to stay under the radar. You might be totally forgotten, overlooked, and passed by when openings develop elsewhere in the organization or when promotions are to be handed out within your own operation. Some folks say, "I want to get lost on the company," or "leave me alone just to do my job." With this attitude, a person might slide along throughout an entire career, doing whatever job had been assigned and making no waves until the gold watch time arrived along with a pension (if the organization had one) and Social Security. Some people try to stay under the radar, all the time planning their next move, and hoping not to be noticed until that great new opportunity comes along. There's nothing really wrong with this strategy assuming the opportunity that was expected actually developed.

Steve, an Associate Professor at a highly regarded southern public university, did his heavy post-graduate work at two universities in the western part of the United States, all the while being alert for a possible position at the southern university of his choice. This particular university had a thriving department in his chosen field. So he stayed in the west working quietly and efficiently, and keeping his head down for several years. He remained hunkered down, doing his work, avoiding any possible upwards movements which would have tied him at least semi-permanently out west, but with his senses sharpened to any possible opening in his dream university. Viola! It arrived! An opening came and he quickly accepted the appointment, moved east and south, developed a strong following among students and gained the respect of his colleagues. After several years he became Assistant Chair in a thriving department of 25 faculty colleagues. He purposely stayed below the radar during his time in the west, working quietly and diligently awaiting for the ultimate opportunity which, in fact, did arrive.

Don't necessarily bet your career on "the call" finding you under the radar such as happened to Steve in the previous paragraph. While you remain more or less anonymous under the radar, you will still need to develop alliances to help you with your personal objectives—whether they be to remain as you are and ply your trade quietly and out of sight, or to keep on the lookout for the next great opportunity which may or may not come. You will never go wrong with alliances. Alliances will help you move up and out. But, if you choose to remain where you are, more or less under the radar, alliances will also add strength and stability to the job you are doing in the unit of your choice. It cannot be repeated and emphasized enough that good alliances will always help you along whatever path you choose throughout your career.

An outstanding example of being under the radar for a long stretch and then catapulting into the spotlight was former President of the United States (from 1953-1961) and General of the Army Dwight David Eisenhower. A 1915 graduate of the U. S. Military Academy at West Point, NY, he was 61st academically out of a total class of 164 graduates. No big academic achievement. During World War I he remained in the United States at a training site and attained the rank of captain. During the decades between World War I and World War II, most of the U. S. military was under the radar since the country was intensely involved with the free and easy lifestyle of the "roaring twenties" followed by the dramatic plunge of the nation's economy during the Great Depression of the thirties. Eisenhower was moved around among many assignments during those decades and didn't become a full colonel until 1941—a full 24 years following his promotion to captain!

But after all those years under the radar, the beam finally picked him up and he was forever destined to remain in the spotlight until his death in 1969. Three months after becoming a colonel he was made Chief of Staff of the 3rd Army and became Brigadier General in September 1941, Major General in March 1942, and became Head of Operations of the War Department. In June of 1942, General George C. Marshall, Army Chief of Staff, selected him over 366 more senior officers to be commander of the U. S. troops in Europe. And, as they say, "the rest is history." Obviously, wartime brings all the military into the limelight, but Eisenhower is the brightest example in modern military history of a person moving along quietly under the radar until he exploded like the Fourth of July fireworks into permanent leadership of both the military and the entire nation as the 34th president. While staying under the radar, you run the risk of not being noticed when the next opportunity arrives. During the research for this book, I did not interview one person who had purposely remained under the radar and lived to become disappointed by a missed opportunity. Perhaps no one admitted it or perhaps I just missed finding such persons. But the risk is there and while staying under the radar, you will always need to quietly and carefully extend your antennae to see what's happening around you—for good or bad. In any job or position, no matter what your work includes, and no matter what level of employment you find yourself, it is absolutely essential that you remain aware of your environment and of all activity that might have a bearing on your job or your future.

LESSON VIII: Staying under the radar can afford you the opportunity to do your job quietly end effectively. It can shelter you from turmoil that may be developing around you, but it also may eliminate you from new opportunities if you remain silent and invisible. While choosing to stay under the radar, you must nevertheless be fully aware of conditions around you that may or may not impact your work and your future. Be prepared to let the radar beam pick you up when conditions are in your favor and when you are picked up, be prepared for the consequences.

CHAPTER NINE

AND THE CULTURE UPSTAIRS

I was involved with a small not-for-profit institute that defined itself as a research center studying aspects of the mind associated with processes outside of the physical realities of human experience—in other words, extra-sensory perception and the like. A six person staff managed the day by day operations of the center, including creating, finding funding for, and conducting carefully controlled testing of individuals who were often the subjects of this scientific research. The organization was overseen by a 15 person Board of Directors, headed by a President. Here's where the culture of the Board upstairs and the culture of the staff clashed—and it had clashed during the seven or eight years that I had been personally involved as a Board member.

The Board historically met only once each year, but a local Executive Committee of the Board usually met monthly. The Executive Committee had the support of the Board and was able make most decisions necessary for the ongoing functioning of the organization. The staff, on the other hand, paid the bills, did the research, managed an extensive library, made local contact, did more fund raising than the Board (which had more or less ignored this important responsibility), held regular research and educational events for the public, and felt a proprietary ownership of the center, even though the Board was the legal owner.

Therefore, when instructions, policy implementations, changes in direction, etc. came from the Board, the staff would often bristle and head toward open rebellion. The staff had asked for representation on the Board in an attempt to keep the lines of communication parallel, but this did very little to soften the conflict between the staff and the board upstairs. Over the years, things became so ruffled that in the face of a major drain on the center's assets, a portion of the staff was terminated, others took reduced hours and salary, and the Board had to pony up substantial dollars employing a fund raising professional in an attempt to replenish the diminished endowment. All this actually resulted from a long-standing difference in management understanding and techniques between the Board (the culture upstairs) and the staff. Non-profit organizations have continuing management issues, usually grown out of a shortage of funds. Since most non-profits receive their operating income from membership dues, or from services they sell, or from the goodwill of donors, they often receive enough suggestions on managing that could litter the bridal suite with rose petals. This fund raising pattern will always create tensions between the paid staff and those upstairs on the Board.

Other differences were quite obvious in a position I once held in a large New York City insurance brokerage firm. I discussed in Chapter Three the difficult situation of my not being fully aware of the expectations for me in a new position. That was the same firm in which I will now discuss the differences between my understanding of my responsibilities and job requirements compared to the perceived objectives of those above me (upstairs). I was busy building an effective staff and attempting to give each of them meaningful employment as well as fair compensation. One day I was called into the President's office and told that I had too much overhead cost which included excessive salaries. I knew from careful research that the salaries of my staff were at least in line with others in similar positions in the city, and in some cases, actually lower than the market was paying. I was stunned! The President was known to have very little use for the type of insurance my staff sold and serviced (employee benefits) and therefore was not interested in giving me adequate support. On the other hand, the Chairman of the Board of the company liked our specialty products and gave us the needed support to continue on with our plan of operations. I was caught between a President who insisted that I reduce some salaries and a Chairman who supported things as they were. In this situation, there were obvious basic differences between my objectives and those of at least one senior officer, and, at the same time, there were culture differences between the two top officers of the firm.

This is the worst possible situation—two senior officers, both of whom could have pulled whatever strings they wished, differing in the support of an operating department. Those "on the line" will be forced to listen to both opinions and often to differing sets of instructions, and be forced to negotiate the tightrope stretched between the two senior officers. Let me tell you, this is an untenable situation. The line manager will need to remain close to the supportive senior and, at the same time, attempt to develop a better understanding of work with the non-supportive senior. Persuasion will produce minimal results. Negotiation will also have little effect. I have found that the only foolproof way to convince the negative executive would be through better than average performance.

In my case, performance saved the day. I was able to develop a solid relationship and some new revenue from the unsupportive senior's favorite account—a large New York bank. I found myself attending lunches, going to inter-company meetings, and having after work drinking bouts with some of the client's staff. The unsupportive senior probably didn't fully come around, but when he saw positive results from my involvement with his favorite account, he quieted down and let me manage in the manner I had programmed. Survival when faced with any unsupportive executives upstairs is best assured by performance above and beyond established expectations. If the executive upstairs fails to notice and appreciate such exemplary performance, survival is unlikely.

In other situations, even solid performance may not be the key to unlocking a ruptured relationship between those upstairs and yourself. This is where some alliances will be essential. There always will be someone or several individuals who have both the ear and the trust of every senior officer or manager. This may be someone's secretary, an employee with a long history, but in a non-sensitive position, or a mid-level manager with whom you have become friendly. You need to work diligently to develop a trusting friendship with these persons. You can do this by being especially friendly, offering to assist on a particularly troublesome project, join them at a casual lunch, and gradually develop a fairly strong and trusting relationship. It will only be after trust has developed that you will be able to prevail upon them to intercede for you upstairs. If there is no trust, there can be no help. After the trust has been given birth and your new ally has created an opening for you, from then on you are flying solo.

You will need to know what differences in culture, both physical and attitudinal, that there might be between you and those above you. In the first place, those who dwell upstairs live in a different physical environment than you do. Senior officers have "guard dogs"— secretaries or administrative personnel who's job is to keep the riff-raff away from the door. Sometimes these "guard dogs" can be seduced, professionally, that is, by quiet conversation, occasional tokens of mutual interest (news clippings, sports items, etc.), notes of good cheer, or just by letting them know that *you know* that they maintain control of this rarified environment. You may have an administrative or secretarial person at your level of work who has already become a friend of the boss's secretary. You can readily use this friendship as a door opener to see the boss. But when you are confronted by the boss's secretary, show courtesy, humility, and have a professional bearing. Soon enough you will know that this guardian in this rarified atmosphere, is willing, and possibly anxious, to become "one of the boys (girls)" along with the rest of you.

In my first significant job, my boss's boss had a secretary who appeared formidable and almost cruel. But by careful respect and later learning we had some common history, she melted nicely and became a friend. The most helpful reward you can have by cultivating the trust of these guardians will be the tips they might offer as to the best techniques to assure affirmative responses from the bosses. With these techniques in hand, when you reach the desk of the senior officer or manager, the differences between what you are requesting and what you expect the senior to offer are perceived to be much greater than reality. One or two meetings, with your bringing along adequate and accurate supporting information, may pave the way for understanding and support.

But other times you will quickly learn that the upstairs culture is definitely heading in a direction substantially different than your plans, hopes, or expectations. This puts you in the face of crunch time. You will need to either buy into what you have learned upstairs and plan to conform, or continue in the direction you are heading (very risky) and hope performance will bring the two differing cultures closer. Or you may be forced to head for the door. Please be fully aware that continuing along your track while *knowing full well that your direction differs from the direction being set upstairs* will likely lower your standing in the organization and possibly lead to a forced demotion or termination. "Them's the bosses, and you'd better pay attention!"

In some cases differing cultures can eventually blend and give support toward a healthy growth of the organization. My first job of any significance was with a large and prestigious insurance company in Hartford, Connecticut. I was employed in the Group Insurance Department which at that time was somewhat new and rather a stepchild in comparison to the well-established Individual Insurance operation that had a historical and respected reputation of dealing with the wealthy, and producing substantial profits for the company. The upstairs culture accepted "Group" but was wary and anxious as to the long term viability of the upstart.

The company sold Individual Insurance in large amounts to wealthy business owners and professionals. "Group", on the other hand, dealt with businesses and sold handfuls of small amounts of insurance to bunches of employees. As time went on, however, conditions changed and "Group" grew quite rapidly. The folks upstairs began to soften and even began to realize that the growing adolescent was becoming an important contributor to the welfare of the organization. The cultures blended! Then in about another 15 years, the company realized that "Group" was the driving culture of the moment and for the future, so the old "Grand Dame" of the company, the Individual Insurance operation, was actually jettisoned—sold to another competing organization. In this example, the upstairs officers, from an older and more established culture, were willing to support a newer and growing product line which eventually became the recognized trademark of the institution which by then had created its own unique culture.

Even the physical environment of the upstairs crowd presents the image of a different culture from the operating units. I once visited the office of a vice president of Metropolitan Life Insurance Company in New York. This officer, who was not even in the highest echelons of company management, had an outside receptionist's office, an interior secretary's office the size of a large bedroom, and then the vice president's personal office, almost as large as the Oval Office of the President of the U. S. It even had a working fireplace. I wasn't employed there but I was certainly awe struck by the size and trappings of it all. But can you imagine how a junior underwriter or claim representative within the Metropolitan Life would react being ushered into such a Taj Mahal? There just can't possibly be a meshing of cultures when senior personnel surround themselves with immense luxury and then expect junior staffers to jump onto the band wagon of ideas or directives coming from upstairs.

Some of the high flying technology companies of the 1980s and later were founded by men and women who often let their ego's direct some of their interests and habits. For example, according to *Fortune Small Business Magazine* of March 2003, Larry Ellison,

CEO of Oracle Electronics, had a $100 million Japanese imperial style residence; enjoyed flying his plane, an Italian fighter jet; piloting his yacht; and enjoying his Icelandic pony and cats. How would a mere mortal employee living in a three bedroom house and driving a Ford Taurus handle a confrontation or interview with such a person who also was known to have assets exceeding $15 billion? These cultures would just not blend.

Some senior executives either are or just appear to be somewhat embarrassed by luxury, new wealth, and mammoth executive suites—especially if they have recently arrived there and have been pulled away from the day to day operations where their diggings were more humble. But don't be fooled. The regal comforts, the "guard dogs," and all other significant support so common in the upstairs environment, can quickly become routine to the executive. It's quite pleasuresome to slip into the country club life and to enjoy sitting in first class sections while flying commercial aviation (if one doesn't have his own plane).

Sometimes you will be called to appear in these stratospheric environs. The first thing to remember is not to look around in wonder or comment loudly about the size, furnishings, or other luxuries of this higher-up individual. You might have been a friend and close working associate of this executive who has recently been promoted upstairs, so the best conversation starters might be to joke politely about your friend's new digs, even if he or she might now be your boss and not an equal associate, as in the past. All in all, however, you need to take this environment for what it is, enjoy your visit, and then scamper happily to your own cubicle where you still work and feel comfortable.

On the other hand, you need to accept the comforts of senior trappings. You might have a job where you need to interact with the upstairs people on a regular basis. In that case you will need to make friends and gain the trust of the "guard dogs"—the secretaries and receptionists who set appointments and usher in lower staffers and outside visitors. Knowing and having the trust of these loyal and highly-paid guardians of the upstairs can get you early admission, convenient appointments, and sometimes personal e-mails and cell phone numbers not known to the outside world. And you'd also be surprised how business plans or ideas of yours can be moved along in your direction if key secretaries and administrative assistants know what you're hoping for and will pass along a good word to their bosses in your behalf.

Senior executives receive information and ideas from many sources and often don't have the time or inclination to review everything in full detail. They do review in detail topics that have a definite bearing on their own fiefdom, particularly bearing on financial results, but other recommendations, processes, or ideas which don't have immediate impact often are put on the bottom of the pile. That's where the help of a strong ally who is a secretary or other type of support staff to the seniors might move your project along toward a favorable decision. Remember that strong and trusting alliances are essential for any survival in the corporate world.

AND REMEMBER THAT SOME DAY YOU MIGHT BE THE SENIOR EXECUTIVE.

LESSON IX: When dealing with those upstairs, always realize that the upstairs culture will almost often differ in varying degrees with your work day culture. Learn to understand the upstairs culture and attempt to develop allies who will enhance your relationships with senior personnel. Respect the differences between your cultures and theirs but learn to deal with these differences in a respectful and accepting manner.

CHAPTER TEN

CAUGHT IN AN OVERNIGHT CULTURE CHANGE

In 1923, Henry R. Luce co-founded *Time Magazine* and incorporated Time, Inc. During his 40 some years at the helm, Luce built a corporate and editorial staff of patrician white males, many of them from Princeton University, and sold magazines to an audience of similar types. Jobs in the growing Time, Inc. empire were stable, and as openings developed within the organization, most available positions were filled by those within the family. Even as recently as 1998, "the heirs to particular jobs were predictable and long apparent." (This quote and much of the information in this chapter about Time, Inc. is from a *New York Times* article of May 11, 2003.)

When management employed Norman Pearlstine in 1995 to become Editor in Chief of Time, Inc., things changed very little. Editors of the various magazines were replaced only as needed and the culture remained generally calm and collegial. With 125 magazine titles and earnings before interest, taxes, depreciation and amortization at $1.155 billion in 2002, Time, Inc. remained a dynamic revenue producer for the parent company, AOL Time

Warner. But as David Carr, the *New York Times* reporter who did this story on Time, Inc. said, "Time, Inc. was the equivalent of an editorial civil service, a model of stability and, some would say, provincialism."

Suddenly, in July 2001, Mr. Pearlstine put power in the hands of John Huey, promoting him from running the company's business magazines to the position of Editorial Director for all of Time, Inc. In less than one year under Huey's direction and with Pearlstine's approval, editors at eight major Time, Inc. magazines were replaced by editors outside the specific magazines and, in four instances, by editors from outside Time, Inc., an unheard of attack on the old Luce culture. Included in the Pearlstine-Huey team was Isolde Motley, the Corporate Editor. According to some Time, Inc. editors and others within the organization, "the high-tempo, high-risk upheavals have shaken the corporate culture, alienating some talented Time, Inc. editors and writers who wonder if the focus on new blood will drain their careers of promise." A former managing editor of *Sports Illustrated* Mark Mulvoy said, "The whole culture has changed. All of the magazines now look the same, and the editors have become faceless, interchangeable people. A lot of the direction for the magazines is coming from upstairs, not the individual editors."

Even though the share price of the parent, AOL Time Warner, plummeted shortly after the merger of America On Line and Time Warner took place in 1999, the business value of Time, Inc. continued to grow and through 2002 had shown 11 years of continuous earnings growth. But the sudden explosion of culture, facilitated by Huey and Motley, sent some people packing, made others literally quake from head to toe, and left the rest with a feeling of unease. So how does a person survive while this cultural upheaval is rumbling like summer thunder throughout the organization?

The publishing business is not a high margin enterprise and over the decades, mergers and acquisitions have changed its face dramatically. Publishing companies (both magazine and book) have been bought and sold; some have been combined with radio and television conglomerates; others have tried to re-make themselves and follow current trends. Many old line American companies are now owned by mega-corporations from Europe and elsewhere. Nevertheless, there are ways individual employees can survive within the profession if they are deft and diligent.

In a situation like the sudden culture shift at Time, Inc., the individual editors who were most visible were the first targets, as was mentioned above. There survival rate would be best assured by good financial results of their individual magazines. While editors were responsible for content and not advertising sales or marketing, the content of their journals would have had a strong bearing on sales results and the financial health of their property. Thus, if their magazine was producing adequate bottom line results, they would have been more likely to survive than their neighbor who might have been financially marginal. So as the Huey-Motley team started taking the rolls of the Time, Inc. family, the editors who saw red or even pale pink in their financial results should have been cleaning out their desks and calling their friends in other publishing houses looking for possible openings.

If you look at the masthead (usually columnar lists in the early pages of a magazine naming most of the individuals from the top down who put the magazine into print) of any magazine you will see on one list the editorial staffers, including Managing Editor, Executive Editor, International Editor, Editors, Senior Writers, Writers, columnists, Photography Staff, Art Staff, and other specialties in the world considered "editorial." An additional masthead will list the business, or publishing names such as Publisher, President, Director of Finance, Advertising Sales Staff, Business Office Staff and on and on.

When you, with your eyes or fingers, drift down the list, you will discover an increasing degree of survival as the positions become less visible. The survival message in the publishing world is that if a person is a journeyman staffer (writer, editor, photographer, sales rep, office employee) their survival rate is much higher than those who run the shows. This should not discourage anyone from going after the top jobs. After all, they offer prestige, money, challenging work, and great connections so long as people striving for or already in these top jobs realize that their life expectancy in these positions could be relatively short. Before long they'll be sending e-mails throughout the world looking for "the New New Thing." For most publishing employees the advice for you is no more extensive than advice for individuals in other industries, non-profits, universities, and more: stay focused on your own responsibilities and opportunities and always continue to create helpful and trusting alliances.

One characteristic to be aware of in the corporate world is that senior executives often have very little patience. When a product is brought on line or a new service is offered and if the sales results are slower than hoped for, executives often lose patience, pull the product and fire the people responsible for the poor results. And there is no more immediate change in the culture than being fired! Following such a blood bath, new people are brought in, other innovations are offered the marketplace, with new expectations, and also with possibly unsatisfactory results. This is not to say that hasty decisions are not sometimes good and proper on occasion, but compulsive impatience will disturb all employees, usually cost money in the long run, and lower the confidence level in which the executive had been held.

Here is a startling example of a series of cultural changes created by an impatient executive with whom I was well acquainted. Immediately after I began work in my first New York City job, the company's chief executive died and was replaced by the number two man—a gentleman who had grown up in the sales side of the industry. Starting right after he was made CEO, all of us in the firm were subjected to a series of overnight culture changes which left our heads reeling. I had a satisfying and challenging mid-level management position, reporting to two long-time, respected executives within my product line.

Before I could get fully settled in, BAM! the new CEO had terminated the more senior of these two executives and summarily moved the other to a less prominent position in the firm(see chapter two). BAM!—I then reported to a new company-wide sales executive brought in from the outside. This executive had been brought up in another product line than mine, so I was forced to attempt to blend into his strange and difficult cultural requirements. He lasted, I think, perhaps one year or so and BAM!—was immediately replaced by another outsider with a new bag of cultural tricks which required more learning and blending. Life was very uncomfortable and stressful for me and also for the others who fell into this new person's realm.

The next big culture change came when the CEO went outside once more and BAM—hired a new Chief Operating Officer to have jurisdiction over all company functions. This new, bright executive brought in a raft of operational techniques that threw all departments onto their collective ears. This meant to me that, in the four years I had been working with this company, I had reported to BAM, BAM, BAM, BAM, BAM, BAM!—no fewer than six separate individuals, all of whom had different bags of culture that eventually eroded my position to the point where I bailed out and, as they say, "found another opportunity."

The job that I had was eventually filled by another mid-level executive who rode out the changes in culture, until several years later, was himself fired for offering financially unsound products to the market. This culture shuffle I just described is not typical of many organizations, for such constant upheaval does not bode well for the total organization. In fact, the company where all this culture blasting took place, still exists in name, but was sold to another firm which had been chaired in later years by the COO who had been hired to manage the organization I worked for. Therefore, as the scenario played out, the COO of the firm I was with moved on to bigger and better things and then turned around and bought out his old boss. As they say, "what goes around, comes around."

When these culture shifts drop out of the blue, there is some defense for most folks, except those who worked closely with any executive on the way out and who supported his/her policies. If you were a staffer of the soon-to-be-jettisoned executive, your best bet would have been to follow him/her out the door and hope a job will come for you when the executive finds the next employment. Others who might be able to survive the swinging pendulum of culture changes need to remain focused on their own occupations, keeping in mind that while culture upheavals rip through one major operation of the company, they aren't necessarily fatal. After I left this company, I remained close to many former co-workers and I noted with some delight that those who weren't caught in the overnight culture changes and who maintained a diligent pursuit of their own occupations survived quite well and took advantage of the situation when the upheaval subsided. It is important to remember that when these eruptions of culture keep rumbling through the organization, they usually are caused by a few individuals (usually a senior executive) and eventually everyone from the top down will ultimately come to realize that such tremors are not healthy for the entire organization. If an organization gets the reputation of having sudden and massive changes in culture and direction, supporters or investors will fade into the dusk and sources of capital will dry up. When this happens, the organization itself will need to be in a survival mode and in order to survive, things will begin to stabilize.

LESSON X: In some organizations, sudden and dramatic shifts in culture will take place without warning. If you are secure in your job and if you have built effective alliances within the organization, you may likely survive these sudden culture upheavals. If, on the other hand, you are on the wrong side of the sudden changes, you may find satisfaction and more stability elsewhere.

CHAPTER ELEVEN

SO YOU'RE THE NEW CEO

In the summer of 1999, an unknown dynamo direct from Lucent Corporation and formerly from AT & T was snatched by means of a head hunter search to be the new Chief Executive Officer at the old line technology company, Hewlett-Packard (HP). The lady, Carlton (Carly) Fiorina, became an instant celebrity. HP was considered an insular company, satisfied with its own people and not receptive to an outsider, no matter how stellar were the credentials. But not much mattered at that time as the "silicon valley" tech companies were bounding along, producing new and quickly accepted products as their stock prices tipped the stratosphere. HP showed soaring earnings and new highs in the stock price. Even though Fiorina was generally rejected by HP employees, the bright financial results overrode this early rejection.

This courteous, but arranged, honeymoon lasted only until the technology industry bubble burst in late 2000, and along with most all such businesses, HP's financial results began to erode. Fiorina decided that HP needed an overhaul. Despite being highly respected, HP was somewhat slow and plodding and needed a culture transfusion. Fiorina inserted the needle and announced a merger (more like an acquisition) with Compaq Computer for a $19 billion price tag. HP was considered by many to be stodgy; it was controlled by engineers who were careful, orderly, and often considered too slow. Compaq, on the other hand, was a newer go-go company with an upbeat culture created by innovative people.

Fiorina fought hard to get approval for the merger and finally succeeded in ramming it past some reluctant board members. After the deal was signed and the company became known to investors as HPQ, she spent most of her days jetting around the world as a super saleswoman convincing HPQ employees that the merger would work. It was the HP culture that needed a change, not the Compaq culture. Meeting by meeting, strategy session by strategy session, she gradually prevailed. There were thousands of employee shifts and up to 20,000 lay-offs, but Carly Fiorina, by dint of backbreaking schedules and an evangelistic belief in the ultimate worth of the merger, succeeded in putting the two companies together under a much more progressive culture than had prevailed when she became CEO of the old HP. And that, my friends is often the first order of business for a new CEO—revitalize and re-energize the culture of your new employer. Otherwise, why would you have been chosen for this challenging position?

Another high profile CEO was Bill Ford of the Ford Motor Company. No present day American automobile manufacturer has a longer and better known history than Ford Motors—from the day when Bill's great-grandfather, Henry, was to have said, "Tell them they can have any color they want, as long as it's black." But young Bill Ford (45 when he became CEO) never aspired to be the company's CEO. While he had spent 23 years among many Ford jobs, his instincts were elsewhere. But he and the Board of Directors realized that both finances and products were failing, due to poor quality and low morale. The blame was put at the feet of the CEO Bill Ford replaced. With Ford Motors in a deep hole full of poisonous reptiles, young Bill was forced to cut costs (layoffs) and even close some plants. He re-hired several retired and previously successful executives, and then set about to rebuild a culture that he found was laden with pessimism and low morale. With the Ford family still owning 40% of the stock, Bill Ford had not only his employees and products to worry about, but a mountainous amount of family interest.

Young Ford then set about doing much of what Carly Fiorina did—he made himself available. He visited dealers; he showed up unannounced at assembly lines; he met with many managers other than his own direct reports. He zealously moved throughout the company and into Wall Street to brighten up the culture and to shore up investor confidence. While Ford Motor's future is still somewhat uncertain at this writing, Bill Ford, new CEO, correctly set about to replace a culture of pessimism and uncertainty with one focusing on optimism and increased profitability. (The source of much of this information about Ford is from a *Fortune Magazine* article of March 18, 2002, written by Betsy Morris; the Fiorina information is from the same issue, written by Adam Lashinsky.)

There's no getting around the fact that CEO's are set apart from the rest of us. They speak for their companies; they get praise or blame, deserved or not; they sometimes lose control of their power and abuse it flagrantly; they can make substantial contributions both to the culture of their firms and to their communities.

Two very thoughtful and creative authors, Kristine Sullivan, Ed.D, and Johanna L. Howell, interviewed eleven Seattle, Washington CEO's and senior executives and published an illuminating book titled *Wide Awake in Seattle* (the turnaround title came from a popular fictional film story, *Sleepless in Seattle*), published by Integrity Publishing. In the preface of the book, the interviewed executives are described as "the most productive and considerate leaders in Seattle." Each of these leaders had faced many of the challenges experienced by CEO's worldwide: layoffs, restructuring, retraining, re-engineering, and hosts of other cultural and structural changes essential and found in both for-profit and not-for-profit organizations. Throughout these interviews, the CEO's described their approach to empowering employees and developing and using their best abilities. While *Wide Awake in Seattle* was not produced as a text book for business school students, it should be read by future and present CEO's as a practical guide to successful management style and opportunity. The interviews all explored graphic examples of how employee empowerment and other positive management innovations led to valuable programmed results for each of the executives' organizations.

As a vivid example of how empowerment can work, Philip Condit, before he became CEO of Boeing Aircraft, headed the project specifically created to develop an entirely new airplane—the Boeing 777. He decided at the outset of the project to engage more people in the process—more people than had worked on other such projects—and to have them working in teams. This empowerment process got people taking his original thinking, refining it, and adopting it as their own. "The project gradually belonged to all of us," said Condit. The mission statement for the 777 thus became "working together to produce the preferred new airplane." This concept of working together was such a significant success that it ultimately became part of the common culture at Boeing.

In the overall handling of their obligations and responsibilities, CEO's need to be especially aware, regularly examining their terrain and their own home base. They can be hurt by sudden shifts in the culture around them without having done any wrong! When a strong executive, Walter Wriston, retired as CEO of the huge New York Citibank, his chosen successor was John Reed. Reed was more studious, more deliberate, and less charismatic than Wriston and stayed out of the media limelight except when necessary.

After several years at the helm, a fast moving merger-driven executive, Sanford (Sandy) Weill, managed to create a mega-financial organization by merging his Travelers Insurance Company into a newly incorporated CitiGroup which included Citibank as well as Salomon, Smith Barney, a Wall Street investment firm. Before the amalgamation into CitiGroup, Weill had brought several pieces from previous mergers into a firm called Primerica which he first had merged into the Travelers. Soon Edward Budd, Travelers

CEO, was gone. Next in line, as Travelers merged into CitiGroup, Weill and Reed became co-CEO's, allegedly with equal power and equal responsibilities. But never with a go-go CEO like Weill around could a person with Reed's style survive the new culture for long. Soon Reed was forced to take the same path taken by Budd—early retirement, but, of course, with a nice golden parachute. Two styles of management, both designed to create contradictory cultures can rarely co-exist in the same organization. The culture with which Reed was comfortable suddenly changed around him, and even though he was talented and respected, he didn't belong with CitiGroup.

A small not-for-profit organization with which I am involved was managed for several years by a very methodical and rather reclusive individual. He was well respected within his profession, but was somewhat insular within the organization that he was hired to manage. He stayed in his private office, working on his computer, doing research, communicating with his chosen associates elsewhere. He preferred to function in partial isolation without interference or direction from his Board of Directors and he preferred to manage his research projects rather than manage his staff. As a not-for-profit, he refused to ask people for money, which as most of us know, is a main element in the job description of an executive in such a position. Suddenly, at an annual Board meeting, a new and somewhat trigger happy Chairman was elected and immediately established "the Board of Directors is now in Control" culture. This new style of Board-induced culture, deemed interference by the astonished manager, was too much for him. He unceremoniously quit. Then, at a safe distance from his former job, he publicly lobbed hand grenades of criticism at the new Chairman and several others on the Board. Suddenly this abrupt culture change was so swift and confrontational, the only survival option for the CEO-manager was to pack up and leave.

In small and unstructured organizations, this type of sudden, disrupting culture explosion is more likely to happen than in a large, layered organization where explosions, while they do happen, tend to be more muffled. Also, such culture "adjustments" often are given a spin by a public relations firm in an attempt to glorify the negative. Thus CEO's in these small and mostly informal organizations need a flexible style of management and, more importantly, need to maintain tight control of all the elements that would tend to alter the culture that the manager had created or inherited. In this specific case, the CEO stayed mostly to himself, did not cultivate a solid relationship with his Board members, and thus was a fat target when the new Board Chairman initiated a sudden culture change.

Kevin Sowers was the interim CEO of a large community hospital that was affiliated with the massive and widely respected Duke University Health System. After holding that interim position until a permanent CEO was obtained for this hospital, Sowers then was promoted to become the Chief Operating Officer of Duke Hospital. Duke is known internationally as a superior treatment and research system as well as a teaching hospital. Sowers told me that his job was to make people recognize that what they do was important. In a hospital, employees must understand the needs of patients, the physicians, and the families of patients. As CEO he always recognized with a personal commendation, any employee, be they nurse, physician, orderly, or office administrator when a kind word or thank you had been received from a patient or a family member. This kind of recognition parallels the empowerment strived for by the Seattle executives in *Wide Awake in Seattle*.

Most CEO's are not celebrity CEO's. Most run their organizations by using the skills of their product—grocery knowledge helps the small independent food retailer, restaurant management can be overseen by a creative chef, auto repair shops from a crack mechanic, law offices from a skilled litigator. Very few have studied management. They run their organizations using their product skills while culture builds around them as they try to learn management on the run. The most tragic mistake made by small organization CEO's is not to control the development and growth of the culture in their own shops. Typically, they are so committed and often blinded by their own efforts to build the business and to survive by their own skill and knowledge, they fail to see the creeping and perhaps fatal culture growth in their own organizations.

As an example of creeping, potentially destructive culture, a man I once knew was building a small, independent financial services book of business. The business was growing well, he was attracting new clients, so he felt the need to employ an office administrator. He found a woman recommended by a friend who came from a professional background with product knowledge similar to his own. They worked well together, but gradually, the administrator developed bad habits—over sleeping, drinking too much alcohol, and partying late into the night. The entrepreneur overlooked these habits and even accompanied her through longer and longer lunch hours. He didn't control the culture and it deteriorated around him until it was somewhat controlled by the growing bad habits.

While the business owner saw what was happening, he took a *laissez faire* attitude about the troublesome culture and let things slide along. Soon, however, the business was sold and the first action taken by the new owner was to identify the unhealthy and unproductive culture and send the administrator packing. The new owner CEO thus had the immediate opportunity to establish his own culture on what was a prosperous and growing business—which might have otherwise struggled to keep up the growth that had been created so effectively by the former owner. That, then, is the real opportunity too many new CEO's fail to recognize. Just like Carly Fiorina, they must uproot, and replace a culture going nowhere with a more vibrant and productive culture that all the employees can adopt with some passion. It may take awhile, but it's the answer to survival and success.

LESSON XI: Most CEO's, new to their jobs, very likely will need to change the culture of their organization, often with painful results for some, but hopefully, with positive results for the organization.

The CEO has a wonderful opportunity to develop a trusting and supportive relationship with employees by recognizing their accomplishments and empowering them to be creative and work together for the benefit of all.

No matter how large or small the organization, the CEO must influence the direction of the culture to assure that officers and employees work together to accomplish their common objectives.

CHAPTER TWELVE

YOUR HEALTH IS YOUR LIFE

As you read this chapter, think of those you know, or have heard about, that are living with ill health. If you are young and just beginning your career, remember some of the older folks—friends of your parents maybe, or possibly parents of your friends—or merely names you have heard of those who's livelihoods have been impaired or cut off because of serious medical problems.

Perhaps you are farther along on your career path. You will see around you plenty of fellow workers who are obese, have ailing backs, sore hips, bad knees, are chronically absent, or who have complaints much of the time about allergies, headache, nausea and other assorted aliments.

Now do the research.

A former boss of mine whom I respected and enjoyed working for enjoyed a Coke at his desk along with his morning cigar (before smoking was banned in most corporate environments). For his full lunch, he usually tossed down at least two bottles of his favorite beer. At office social events, he downed more of the same beer. He was likely 80 pounds overweight; other than his daily walks to and from public transport, he followed no plan of exercise. Later in life his health record touched many of the medical specialties—cardiology, oncology, orthopedics, even psychiatry. Believe me, it was tragic to see him disintegrate rapidly just before he retired, and then see his short retirement fill with medical issues prior to an early death.

We live surrounded by clever, sometimes subliminal, encouragement to ingest tokens of physical decline and early death. Recently I purchased a dozen Krispy Kreme glazed doughnuts—the pinnacle product of that creative company's line of tasty baked goods. After eating two of these gems, I decided to look for the nutrition facts on the box. Wonder of wonders! First, the nutritional table was invisible until I found it on the underside of the box—not on either end panel or side panel like most packaged foods where it could easily be studied on the shelf in a food store. When I finally found the news of the food values of each doughnut, I discovered that each single doughnut contained 200 calories—110 of those from fat! One doughnut provided 18% of my daily requirement of fat—15% of the saturated fat allowance. Since all this loaded intake happened before 9:00 a.m. along with the rest of my breakfast, I was deep into my daily calorie and fat allowance—with lunch, possibly cocktails, and dinner down the road. And this wonderfully tasting Krispy Kreme product is only one of hundreds of tempting and tasty food items that induce us to enjoy them by means of their clever advertising, their interesting purchase bargains (coupons, etc), and gobs of pleasure in the joy of eating them.

All this is to say that diet can be a major cause of bodily malfunctions at any time during our lifetimes. Overweight and obesity seem to create a predictable pattern leading directly to various disabilities. Often the first ailment to demand attention with obese people is a faulty and overused gall bladder. A function of this organ is to assimilate fat in the digestive process and when years of excess fat attack the gall bladder, the over worked and pained organ cries out to be yanked.

Next in this predictable pattern of illnesses resulting from obesity might be diabetes—a controllable, but incurable malady that requires life long, somewhat costly, medication. Diabetes itself can lead to vision problems, circulation problems often resulting in limb amputations, and other tragic health problems. And next—how many overweight folks have you known who complain about sore backs, hips, or knees? People with normal weight can go through life without facing the orthopedic knife, but the overweight crowd is a good candidate for corrective or replacement surgery. The artificial hips and knees are wonderful, but why remain overweight, asking for a new joint, when your own, if treated well throughout your life, work even better than the store-bought variety?

If people haven't been tripped up by the above listed maladies, then high blood pressure and/or heart and artery problems will be on this predictable schedule of doom. Now, to those of you who are overweight or obese who dare to read this chapter, don't come up to me and say, "well, these problems won't happen to me. I'll eventually lose this weight and be fine." Your good intentions will be crushed under your own excess weight and, unless you take immediate weight control action, this pattern of physical decline is as predictable as the morning sunrise.

I doubt anyone reading this book is not fully familiar with this pattern of diet related health difficulties. Further, you need only to be barely awake to hear or read about weight loss techniques. Please remember, this is a book about surviving in your employment life and not a weight loss primer or an "eat your way to good health and happy employment" formula. But here are two simple (and not too difficult to follow) guides to weight survival while working: 1) Learn your correct weight for your height and age, and 2) If you are regularly ten or more pounds above the desirable, visit a nutritionist and follow the prescribed eating and exercise program. It won't be long before you will look better, feel better, become healthier and fully removed from the problems outlined above.

That's all you need do. Don't try to cut calories, restrict fatty foods, or create your own diet. Also, avoid weight loss classes, weight loss books, and various well advertised programs. While it's true with weight loss classes you have the support of your fatty peers, but with a nutritionist you have the support of a sympathetic and trained professional, dealing with you one on one. You have a person skilled in his or her methods which, if followed, are guaranteed to produce the desired results. A trained nutritionist will give you all the correct and necessary guidance you will ever need. You will be thrilled (!) as you see the pounds disappear, your waist shrink, and notice that your back pain begins to disappear. With a trained nutritionist you may continue eating many of the foods you enjoy, but the quantities and patterns will change according to your own prescribed program. A nutritionist creates a program specifically for each individual patient, and if followed, the results will amaze you. I should know. It worked well with me and I know where my nutritionist is should I need her again for a refresher program.

Humans are a social breed and enjoy each others company—especially along with a cocktail, a few beers, or a glass or two of wine. In my 40 year experience of life in the corporate world, I witnessed how alcohol could reduce survival chances more predictably and more devastatingly than most other temptations. After World War II when the service professions expanded rapidly—advertising, public relations, financial services—the "two martini" lunch in a white collar urban environment became kind of a generic phrase for alcohol and too often became part of the job. To a great extent, as this book is being written, the "two martini" excess has been replaced by iced tea, soft drinks, or perhaps one glass of wine. But nevertheless, alcohol can enter into the survival struggle.

An old friend and former business associate of mine was a hard-working and well-liked sales professional in the financial services world. He was a jolly Irish-American who always was eager and willing to "toss down a few." People, usually other men, enjoyed drinking with him for the talk usually drifted to one sport or another. He was a keen follower of many teams and an occasional bettor of several sports.

When I retired early from my final corporate role, he remained behind, but frequently phoned me about his unhappiness with the way conditions had changed in the big company. After perhaps a year of dissatisfaction, I arranged a new position for him with a major client of mine. He snatched up the job and was well received by his new cohorts. But the honeymoon was short lived. His work habits were erratic and his production level was unsatisfactory. He had a little trick of leaving the coat of his business suit on the back of his chair and disappearing for long stretches of time—perhaps an hour or more. For awhile, his associates thought he might be working with folks in other departments of the company. But no, that could never be verified. What was learned after several months of mystery was that during those coatless hours, he would be outside the office having a drink or two in a neighboring pub. And he knew most of the bar tenders in the neighborhood and they knew him well. Needless to say, after his management discovered how he took his afternoon siesta, his employment with that large institution was abruptly cut short.

Off he went to one or two other employment opportunities until the only source of employment was himself alone. His wife and two young daughters had moved out and he was totally on his own. He borrowed money from friends and family, sought to build his own business, and continued to drink until one fateful day, an alert police officer saw him leave a local pub, get into his car and drive off. The cop pulled him over, checked his blood alcohol, and gave him a summons that led to loss of license and compulsory alcohol treatment classes.

Here he was in a suburban location, trying to develop clients, many of whom were miles from his home, without a car, and attempting to dry out. For a couple of years he rode his bicycle, hired people to chauffeur him in his car, and religiously attended Alcoholic Anonymous meetings. Fortunately for him and his family, the story has a happy ending. After stopping the alcohol intake, he actually did build a business, paid off his many loans, and remained very close to his growing daughters. But as far as his corporate survival, it ended years ago at the bottom of too many bottles.

What are symptoms you might find during a lifetime of work in a community environment? Ignoring for a minute my sermon on the excess of food and alcohol combinations, what other work-related conditions might interfere with your good health while working for a living?

It's not hard to answer those questions for those people, both men and women, working under certain severe and built in dangerous working conditions—underground mining, for example, or highly dust-laden textile shops which may cause lung or breathing problems, or construction jobs that put heavy requirements on joint and muscle use. These and similar jobs can cause all sorts of physical problems, some fully anticipated and understood by the workers themselves. Labor union bargaining and government regulations have helped tremendously to alleviate many of these physical work related hazards. But what about the more subtle and insidious sneak attacks on body and mind within a white collar or sedentary occupation or profession? How do you know what to expect and how do you identify what we shall call "stealth symptoms"? If you have trouble identifying the symptoms, how can you avoid the illness waiting to make its home within you and, further, how can you find a cure or treatment?

Let's look at some things as common as headache, or chronic indigestion, or even insomnia. Most of us have headaches, some regularly, others intermittently, and others have devastating "migraines." There are all sorts of off the shelf pain killers that are as much a part of the 21st century American diet as Coke or Pepsi. Other "stealth symptoms" include nausea, depression, insomnia, and fatigue or weakness. There are medications for these—some off the shelf such as Pepto Bismol and Nytol. We all know what these medications are and how we react to many of them. Some of these symptoms require a doctor's prescription to assure effective treatment. But then, there are other accepted therapies for these symptoms including many holistic herbal treatments that in come cases perform better that the pharmacy shelf products or even the prescribed pharmaceuticals.

Joe Graedon and Teresa Graedon, Ph.D., have written a book taken from their popular radio show, *The Peoples' Pharmacy.* Their

Guide to Home and Herbal Remedies offers sound and proven advice on using non-conventional herbal treatments. Most traditional physicians stick with medications made by the pharmaceutical manufacturers, so to learn about herbal treatment, you need to do your own investigations. There are multiple sites on the internet describing herbal concoctions, their use and their side effects, if any. In another realm, there are more "spiritual" treatments that include meditation, yoga, and various methods of touch therapy (my choice). There are classes, books, and countless media articles to guide those who seek spiritual help for either physical or mental suffering.

These "stealth symptoms" are primarily caused by stress. Medical studies have shown time after time that conditions such as cancer, cardiac problems and even physical pain can often be a direct result of all kinds of stress—job, home difficulties, and financial problems being the most direct villains of stress-related symptoms. A dear friend called with the alarming news that she recently found a suspicious lump in a breast. She has a very stressful and physically demanding profession, is helping her highly-charged husband overcome severe psychological and alcohol problems, has a daughter who struggled through adolescence and young adulthood and still struggles as an unplanned mother and who is living far from home. Are these stressful issues a cause for her frightening lump? We would all shake our heads and wish that her life conditions were more peaceful and without this overload of stress. But, like many of us, she chose her profession, she chose her husband, and she did her best to raise her struggling daughter. Medication sometimes helps, but seeking an inner peace within one's own body and spirit seems to provide more answers for a great many stress-laden folks. This book is not designed to offer either medical or spiritual help, but merely to point everyone toward the many opportunities that abound to help people maintain, or at best, regain lost health in order to survive on the job.

Moses Maimonides (1135-1204) was the most famous Jewish philosopher of the Middle Ages and became the court physician in

Egypt. In his famous Medical Oath and Prayer he said, "Grant me strength, time and opportunity always to correct what I have acquired, always extend its domain, for knowledge is immense and *the spirit of man can extend indefinitely to enrich itself daily* with new requirements." Like this wise and famous man, we need the strength to make our corrections and use the immense knowledge available so our spirits can extend indefinitely to "enrich life daily."

LESSON XII: Any job, whether it be your life's chosen career or a temporary stop on the way, will be all around more successful if you are within your body's prescribed weight. If you are not, your survival depends upon taking steps to lose the excess pounds. Next, alcohol or other substance addiction will guarantee either a reduction in responsibility or the sunset of survival.

With weight and substance abuse under control, the other hazard to survival is stress. Medical or herbal therapy may help stress related "stealth symptoms", but the surest answer to reducing stress involves some effective spiritual involvement that helps separate the pain from your body and pull away the pressures within your mind.

CHAPTER THIRTEEN

DODGING THE PINK SLIPS

Where you happen to be in what particular industry or profession has a great deal to do with the stability of your job. For example, *The Coloradon* of January 28, 2003, reported that the merger (or acquisition) by Hewlett Packard with Compaq saved overall $651 million, $257 million of that from around 17,900 job cuts. Many of these cuts were from overseas locations, but also many were domestic. If you happened to be the target in the gun sight, your chances of survival did not exist. When improving corporate earnings are paramount, pink slips fill the air like unwelcome hailstones. Also, high risk organizations often fail, which puts an entire work force on the unemployment line. When a company named PillowTex, makers of bed and bath linens, closed in 2003, more then 7,000 workers were told their jobs had ended because the company couldn't compete with international manufacturers that made the same products, but with lower costs. It was too risky for PillowTex to stay in business in the U. S.

Within companies, newly created jobs even in a stable organization can be cut if management becomes disenchanted with the results. Managements often aren't willing to allow enough time for new operations to take hold, mature, and produce profits. When managers see red ink from any losing project, it takes more than the usual amount of courage to hang on until profits are generated—or until it is proven without question that the project will remain a loser. On the other hand, bankruptcies themselves don't always lead to total shutdowns. Often when many employees are shown the door, others are needed to assist with a reorganization and to help manage a leaner and hopefully more solid company in the future.

In the American employment economy of the early 21st century, jobs relating to personal safety and security provided rapidly growing employment. Jobs guarding the public welfare blossomed after terrorists destroyed the World Trade Center in New York on September 11, 2001. Property security guards, airport security jobs, local police officers, and other similar occupations saw absolutely no pink slips and, on the contrary, saw many new positions created. Sudden and substantial funding from the Federal Government helped find and train men and women into these newly created or expanded positions. An almost paranoid fear of terrorists permeated society and all levels of government felt compelled to extend new and enhanced citizen protection. The direct opposite of pink slips—expanded employment—filled the ranks of the security craft. Of all job classifications, security jobs were the most secure and void of pink slips.

Even deep in the culture of old line and apparently solid companies, the culture therein won't necessarily protect employees from pink slips. Testimony to this can be seen from the previous chapter where we discussed the culture change promoted by Carly Fiorina at Hewlett Packard and by Bill Ford at Ford Motor. Part of a drive toward new and more productive cultures in each of these organizations led to cost cutting and a flurry of pink. In this kind of drastic action, terminations often are felt throughout the entire company and hiding from the sharp scalpel of termination can be difficult—often impossible.

The best and most obvious advice anyone can give to avoid pink slips is to be vitally efficient in your work so that your worth is easily recognized. Here are two situations where survival was assured in one and lost in the other. Both were sales positions—easy to monitor through the obvious results of their sales efforts.

My friend, Bill Gulino, was a talented and well known musician in the New York City area. He played with groups, played on the radio and in television, and had performed earlier in his career on cruise ships. But like many musicians, his work was often intermittent, so he needed full-time regular employment (a "day job," as people in the performance world call it) with a steady income to support his life style and his family. Through an uncle who owned a corrugated box manufacturing business, he learned the ins and outs of that business and started selling boxes to businesses needing such packaging material. Working in a family-run business, however, was kind of rocky. Other employees were jealous of his family connections, so it seemed best for everyone that Bill should resign. He worked for awhile with another firm, then finally settled in with a large, well respected regional company. At the two earlier jobs he had learned all there could be learned about corrugated boxes—their chemical make-up, the strengths of various weights of boxes, how they needed to be stored to protect their life expectancy, and what type box fit what end user. Best of all he had a charming, up front personality enjoyed by his customers, so this combination of knowledge and personality along with ability to provide service to his customers when called for, fully guaranteed his survival. His employer had offered high-level management jobs as further rewards, but he graciously declined. He was a highly respected salesman of corrugated boxes, well paid, and still had time to practice his first love—music. He never saw a pink slip nor would he ever so long as the company continues to operate.

Another friend, Bruce, was an account person in a small employee benefit consulting business. He had years of experience and a successful sales record in previous jobs along with excellent product knowledge. He had been hired by his new employer to bring in new business. He made cold phone calls, wrote pre-sale letters, and attended seminars—all to no avail. He brought almost none of his former clients along and failed to develop other new customers. Management was patient, but after more than a year, the patience evaporated. Neither his respected past, nor his product knowledge, nor even his failed sales efforts could save his job. He received the pink slip and did not survive.

The point of these two examples shows that to avoid the feared pink slip, you need to have your arms fully around your job, combining both knowledge and performance. Bill did, Bruce did not.

You remember in Chapter Five we were encouraging carefully arranged alliances? Along with product knowledge and performance, this is a proven technique for use in avoiding the pink slips. This brings me back to my friend Charlie from Chapter Eight who was a master at staying under the radar. Throughout all the mergers and downsizings he and his staff were exposed to, not one pink slip floated onto anyone's desk in his unit! Over the years, he had crafted two sets of alliances which offered him double protection. Remember, he had started his banking career in the money lending business—which, along with accepting and investing customers' deposits, is any bank's primary function. In that early job, he had made the acquaintance of many other young men and women who grew into management positions with time in grade.

When Charlie moved into the specialty operation that he managed, which, you will remember, was unrelated to traditional banking, he remained friendly with all the other fellows he had started out with. Some of those eventually had responsibility for delivering pink slips following some of the mergers, and they always looked the other way when Charlie's name or unit was mentioned. In addition to all his former co-workers and friends, Charlie had his own direct management on his side. Although his unit was small, it was very profitable and one after the other, his bosses were loathe to deliver any termination notices to a group when things were going well. So in his case, Charlie's alliances were two fold: many of his fellow bankers from his early years as well and strong alliances with his present and former direct bosses. Those of us outside the bank who knew him kept shaking our heads as pink slips were fluttering out of the skies onto many desks—often to those we considered unworthy of such notices, but Charlie's group always escaped the bad news. Charlie and several others from his unit retired early with handsome severance packages; other former staffers who remained employed have been happily reassigned to other meaningful positions within the latest merged bank. That is the story of strong and useful alliances.

Another technique, though requiring some rigorous preliminary sleuthing, will help your potential avoidance of the dreaded termination notice. This requires some careful and discreet inquiries prior to your accepting new employment or prior to accepting a transfer or promotion within your present organization. Below is a checklist of areas to pursue as you try to uncover information that will give you a basic understanding of the potential stability of the job you are about to undertake.

• During a job interview, inquire of the average employment term of existing staff, if any. Do people remain long in the unit? When people leave the unit, are they promoted, or do they voluntarily leave, or just what does motivate a change of personnel? If turnover appears low, your chances of stable employment are better.

• Determine how long the unit or organization you will be working in has been in existence. Is this a part of the organization's strong foundation, or could it be a hastily thrown together unit put together for a temporary reason? This will give you an idea of the relative value of the unit to the larger organization and to your chances of finding a stable job opportunity.

• If you are being interviewed for employment with a not-for-profit organization of any type, try to determine the extent of their funding and whether there is any risk of down sizing or layoffs due to a restricted budget.

• If you are becoming affiliated with a specific product or function in a corporation, try to determine what the demand for the product or function is. I once worked in a firm that made a big fuss about a new financial service for small business owners. A small staff was recruited to manage and market the product. Sales results were slower than anticipated, so the product was pulled and the staff was terminated. It might be fun and challenging to be part of a new product venture, but you need to assess the risk and make your own judgment about the viability of the venture.

• Men and women being recruited for high level corporate or institutional positions are more at risk for early termination than entry level employees. Mostly, high level executives sign employment contracts covering all aspects of their positions, including articles spelling out their termination rights and obligations. For those who aren't being given a contract there should at least be a letter specifying all the terms of employment including a position description, the "rules of the road" in the organization, specifics about compensation and benefits, and enough detail to make one quite secure about accepting the position. With this written document, a pink slip is less likely to be presented because the employer has taken great pains to clarify the position and will have invested time and money to assure the right person has been hired. It starts one out with a solid understanding of the job and the employer.

• We often accept jobs because we have friends in the organization and they aggressively encourage us join them. Why do they recommend this? Are they just hoping to pack the place with friends to make the work environment more congenial? Perhaps they aren't truly the best of friends and merely want to use others newly hired behind them in order to increase their own seniority in case of layoffs or promotions. With too many friends working in one place, management will soon notice that an over-abundance of camaraderie among the staff can contribute to a decline in production. This can bring the threat of pink slips. If you are working with friends, see that the work gets done before the office chatter takes over. Some people I know worked for a small not-for-profit institution. Four of them were close. They ate lunch together, covered for one another during time away from the office, and generally ganged up on the other staff who were outside this friendly loop. Well, as luck would have it, things got tight at the institution and among those in "the gang of four", all but one were handed pink slips. The remainder of the staff, those outside of this friendly loop, but who were the productive backbone within the organization, remained employed. The friendship was so tight that it appeared to management that the level of interest and job performance from the friendly four made them expendable. Don't let that happen to you.

LESSON XIII: The level of performance of your work is the best gauge of remaining employed or receiving a pink slip. Employers loathe firing quality personnel.

Alliances within an organization will help assure continued employment, but you must make the correct alliances. More than one alliance will help and alliances within all levels of management can assure employment stability. Advance research will always help. It won't guarantee lifetime employment, but it will give you additional insight into how the organization views your specific job and the unit through which you will be employed. Don't be afraid to ask questions and get your new job in writing!

CHAPTER FOURTEEN

ALONG CAME THE MEGA-MERGER

Throughout this book there have been references to corporate mergers. Corporate marriages, as well as marriages among other institutions, are as old as institutionalism and they will continue. Philip Morris with Kraft Foods; Allegheny Airlines into US Airways; Manufacturers Hanover Bank into Chemical Bank into Chase Manhattan Bank into J. P. Morgan; Chrysler into Daimler/Benz; New York University Hospital with Columbia-Presbyterian Medical Center; the Presbyterian Church in the U.S. (PCUS) into the United Presbyterian Church in the USA (UPCUSA); Pennsylvania Railroad into the New York Central Railroad into Penn Central and eventually into the Federal Government supported Amtrak. With all these mergers, culture would have been markedly affected, some lives would be uprooted, others spared, often depending upon the luck of the draw.

Nothing presents more difficulty than mergers between religious organizations. Such mergers affect not only disparate cultures, but centuries old entrenched elements of faith and doctrine. As any alert person knows, doctrinaire religious persons are the most difficult to move from their beliefs and, in the cases of the more militant religions, even death will not interfere with doctrine. When the two denominations mentioned in the above paragraph merged in the 1983, the result happened only after years and years of study and consultation. The PCUS, commonly called "the Southern Church," preached a conservative theology and based its teachings on more strict Biblical interpretations than their northern brethren. But UPCUSA was the larger organization, better funded, and with more dynamic leadership. In an effort to bring equality to both groups, each moved their former national headquarters—the UPCUSA from New York City and the PCUS from Richmond, Virginia, to neutral ground in Louisville, Kentucky. After the merger, the impact of the changing culture was felt more in the Southern Church than in UPCUSA and those who were most uncomfortable with northern liberal theology bolted the newly-married denominations and either joined existing conservative groups or formed new splinter Presbyterianism.

This was not a merger that saw a flurry of pink slips like many corporate mergers because members were the most severely affected, not employees. There was some consolidation within the headquarters staffs, but layoffs were gentle and those employees who chose not to move to Louisville were given generous severance arrangements. This was advertised as a merger of equals, when in fact UPCUSA's management and theology gradually became dominant. Unfamiliar beliefs, however, were not forced on anyone; terminations of employment or membership were not requested, but with the culture changes, all accompanied by prayer and consultation, there was some agony of the soul that left a sizable number of long time worshipers stranded who had been asked to accept new doctrine, beliefs, and hierarchical church leadership. Many left the fold. Measuring church membership numbers might be compared to measuring corporate earnings in the business world. By any measure, the merger of these two "mainline" Protestant denominations would be considered statistically unsatisfactory just by looking at the membership numbers. The total membership of the combined churches in 2002 was 2,451,969 and the total membership of the two denominations just before the merger was 3,131,228—a 22% loss of membership. Corporate CEO's would have received their golden parachutes and gilt edged pink slips if earnings declined by similar numbers.

Using this religious organization merger example is a good template of other situations in the not-for-profit community. The Boys and Girls Clubs of America have merged into one organization with an attempt to marry male and female interests into a single culture. Many smaller community organizations that receive funding from local United Ways have been forced to merge. In most cases the organizations have survived, but in all cases certain employees of each did not survive. This is the usual. With the attempt to cut costs, the first casualties from mergers are those who are laid off. While lay-offs create charges against the company's books, lay-offs are the quickest way to show cost savings. Within most large organizations there are hundreds of duplicate positions that can be consolidated and erased. But there definitely are ways to survive some mergers and there are techniques in using your time wisely as you attempt to make other employment arrangements as the merger is unfolding. What I am saying here, and will illustrate below, is to plan an escape if it appears that your job will be swept away resulting from a pending or active merger.

In my case, I managed a department in a financial services organization and the management of my firm made an acquisition of another company in another part of the country. It wasn't exactly a merger, but staff and managers of the newly acquired firm took some leadership roles which affected my department directly. I felt uncomfortable. I was asked about products and systems that were unfamiliar to me, but were actively being marketed and operating in the new company's locale. I was told, "this is how we do things in Nashville and we hope you can do the same in New York." It didn't work out that way. The New York market was more rigid. The products we sold were more structured and more highly regulated. In the South where my new associates worked, things were less regulated and employers had less responsibility to provide certain employee services than in the Northeast. It became apparent that the new managers had little confidence in me and this was sadly borne out when another individual was given management authority over my group. I wasn't given a pink slip, but I felt one might be on the print shop, so I used my time actively in attempting to become employed by a competitor. I knew some of the key people in the competitor firm and started to make appropriate contacts. Shortening what could be a long story, after several interviews over a few months, I was able to move smoothly into a senior position with my chosen replacement company. My technique for survival in the face of a threatening merger or acquisition was to work aggressively seeking another position elsewhere. I survived in a very smooth transition and didn't lose one hour of compensation.

This is one of the most essential pieces of activity anyone needs to enter into when a merger is in the offing or after it has happened. Most employees in any industry or profession know people working elsewhere, and in the same field of work. You make their acquaintance in trade shows, in conferences, through journals or publications, by using the Internet and becoming acquainted through e-mails, or even meeting after working hours in a local pub. We told you in Chapter Five that making alliances in your own organization was an essential element of survival. Well, it's even more essential to make acquaintances, friends, or alliances on the outside to give you greater opportunities to survive the possible, or even likely, merger(s) you will face during a long working life. Even if you don't become involved in merger layoffs, just becoming acquainted with your peers in other organizations can be stimulating. While you probably won't learn trade secrets, you will pick up new ideas, learn some of what's good and bad about life inside the competition and get a flavor of culture where the grass may or may not be greener.

A fascinating tale of merger mania is to review the histories of the New York bank, now named J. P. Morgan Chase & Company. Historically, this jumbo banking institution through some of its antecedents reaches as far back as the 18th century. In 1799,

Alexander Hamilton and Aaron Burr established the Manhattan Company to help with the financial development of New York City. Successor banks to Manhattan merged with the Chase National Bank in the 1950s to form Chase Manhattan Bank. Another ancestor of the present J. P. Morgan Chase & Co. was Manufacturers Hanover (familiarly called "Manny Hanny") that got its start in 1812 as the New York Manufacturing Company, with offices at the corner of Nassau and Liberty Streets in lower Manhattan. This company was part bank, part manufacturing company. The banking part was acquired by the Phenix Bank in 1817 that, in 1911, merged and became the Chatham and Phenix National Bank of New York. The Manufacturers Trust Company actually was born in Brooklyn, moved to Manhattan in 1918, and acquired many small banks until it acquired Chatham and Phenix in 1931. The Hanover ancestor to Manny Hanny was founded in 1851 and helped fund the Civil War for the North. Hanover also had several mergers along the way until 1961 when is officially joined Manufacturers Trust.

Another major element of J. P. Morgan Chase is Chemical Bank, another historic New York bank founded in 1824 as a division of the New York Chemical Manufacturing Company. The manufacturing of chemicals ceased in 1832 and Chemical Bank continued to exist, and existed also through many mergers and acquisitions until Manny Hanny merged into Chemical in 1991. Following this, Chase Manhattan merged into the Chemical Banking Corporation in 1996, and in the year 2000, the family tree from these hundreds of mergers settled into one large mighty oak when they were joined by J. P. Morgan Company into the J. P. Morgan Chase & Co. This created a giant retail bank (the Manny Hanny, Chemical, and Chase banks) combined with the old line investment bank of the House of Morgan—famed for financing the wealthy and mighty ever since J. Pierpont Morgan formed J. P. Morgan & Co. in New York in 1861.

Looking back over the histories of these mergers, the roadsides would have been laden with the outcast employees as each merger created new layoffs. Bringing the time line up to date, when Chase and Morgan merged in 2000, it was announced that there would be

5,000 layoffs. Then, as the stock market declined in 2001 and 2002 and as both sides of the merger were pelted with bad news from several huge clients in severe corrupt financial distress, another 5,000 were sent packing, followed by smaller numbers later on. Fortunately for many of these terminated employees, there was some good news. In the first place, they received acceptable severance packages from their employer. And as the new J. P. Morgan Chase was dusting off its losses from the merger, new banks were opening up on many street corners in New York City. North Fork, a Long Island bank, continued to expand in the city. The Commerce Bank, an innovative and customer oriented bank from New Jersey, entered New York and offered weekend banking hours. Other smaller, local banks were expanding and even Wachovia, after a big merger with First Union of North Carolina, opened an office on the corner of 5th Avenue and 45th Street. Most of the operations personnel terminated by J. P. Morgan Chase would soon be able to acquire similar positions with these local, smaller banks. Even the executives who were let go had little trouble affiliating with other banks in New York.

When the explosive technology dream world downloaded into "who's going under today?" syndrome, thousands of skilled people in that industry were laid off and had no new companies, or even old companies, to turn to. This calamitous downturn affected techies in all areas in the U. S. where technology companies had sprouted. Many folks who were unemployed became "consultants" and made the rounds of the surviving companies looking for contract jobs, just to pay the rent and buy food. In the area of California popularly known as "silicon valley," where many of the tech firms were located, real estate prices began to sag because people were selling their homes and moving to other areas where job possibilities loomed larger than in "the valley." The companies that survived were forced to re-examine their products or services to fit what customers demanded. Too often the high flying tech companies created their exciting products and left the understanding of their effectiveness to someone else—who probably was not fully familiar with the new product. Some products, however, stood both the test of time and the test of usefulness. It was these products that helped many companies crawl over the debris of a severe economic downturn and even gradually begin to hire on some of the skilled, but unemployed, staffers still patrolling the neighborhoods for food and jobs.

Now back to the more relevant bank mergers historically described above. There were some major culture shocks along with the mergers as institutions with very different traditions were joined at the hip and told to work together for the good of the new organization. When Manny Hanny merged with Chemical Bank, the managements of each made a vow that the new affiliation would develop smoothly. Meetings were held among various departments of each bank, prior to the announced merger so that individuals could become acquainted and realize that their opposite numbers didn't have horns. Both banks were strong in the retail (branch banking) side of banking, so their cultures matched quite well.

But a few years later, along came Chase Manhattan—both a retail bank and also an institution with a broad international and more sophisticated culture due partly because the Rockefeller family was part of its historic tradition. Although the CEO of Chase quickly lost his portion of control after the merger, many of the senior management positions went to Chase department heads and the Chase culture strongly flavored the mix. This made it difficult for many of the long-time Manny Hanny and Chemical staffers who suddenly found themselves reporting to managers who came from a culture, perhaps more haughty and insular than their accustomed retail-founded attitudes. After a few years, these differences became lost in the blend to improve performance in all areas until it became obvious that J. P. Morgan & Co. needed a new home and it then was merged into the new Chase.

Morgan, who judiciously avoided retail banking and dealing with commoners, thought their way was the only way as they immediately butted heads with the more eclectic attitudes and traditions from the three banks they were forced to live with. It was a shot gun wedding, to be sure, but the Morgan people did their best to swim on top of the water and not drown with all these retail street workers. To make matters worse, shortly after the merger, the American economy became rather lifeless and at the same time, some of the investment banking deals made by Morgan as well as some Chase deals soured in the face of corporate scandals among several clients. This lead to angry finger pointing and articles in the business press questioning whether the newly-merged titan could survive in its present form. The CEO of the entire operation, William Harrison, was publicly under fire, but struggled diligently to make all remaining parties develop a team attitude and pull together. He went so far as to retain a highly successful college basketball coach, Mike Krzyzewski of Duke University, to motivate the senior managers of the merged giant with a highly charged teamwork message. In spite of the massive layoffs, the striving towards teamwork gradually took hold and the new J. P. Morgan Chase became a force in the financial world and a darling to Wall Street investors.

LESSON XIV: Merged organizations are as common as hay fever and often as troublesome for employees. The best protection for everyone is to make strong and friendly connections with other individuals who work in other organizations, but in your chosen profession or occupation. As merger talk fills the air around you, capitalize on these off-campus friendships to help you arrange a healthy escape route, if needed.

When remaining after the merger documents have been signed and jobs seem more secure, strive mightily to develop a team attitude and don't be dissuaded from working as a team even when teamwork style might be rejected by your newly acquired associates. They'll either come around or they'll disappear out the back door.

CHAPTER FIFTEEN

HOW MUCH CAN YOU TOLERATE?

Surviving in the workplace takes some doing. Surviving often is a more intense challenge than the work itself. We've talked about avoiding the pink slips, making good alliances, dealing with mergers, and other challenges that stretch your abilities to survive. During your struggles to survive, as you pull forward all your resources to make a difficult situation tolerable, just has much longer can you tolerate the situation you now are in? Will conditions improve? What inner strength can you personally call upon to enhance your desire and improve your ability to survive? What is your level of tolerance and what steps should you take to make the situation tolerable? Perhaps you should accept the fact that there will be no improvement and move on to a situation with which you can deal.

When work situations approach an intolerable limit, that translates to *stress!* Stress is a condition that has been written about in almost all popular magazines and even in daily newspapers. Television talk shows all have physicians, psychologists, and other advice givers to warn about stress and offer guidance to avoid or limit stress. It has become the household and work place malady of the 21st century. I spoke with a young man recently who had been chosen to manage a small not-for-profit institution. He had been running a low fever and feeling poorly. I cautioned him to be aware of the stress found in his new position. His surprising response was that he could handle the stress of the job, but he was receiving a dose of stress at home because his wife felt his pay was too low for the new job he had just acquired. Stress lurks in strange places—the shop, the office, often at home and we all try to deal with it in our own bumbling ways. It doesn't hurt to get some practical advice to help soften our stress— no matter what its source.

An article in the March 11, 2003, issue of the *Wall Street Journal* by Jane Spencer said, in essence, that we need to deal with stress while we are actually wallowing in it. She admonished us not to charge ahead in our work, building up more stress as the days and weeks progress, and then mellow out at some spa or health refreshment stand to soften up. No. Her advice is to learn to handle stress as it builds during a work day or night. For example, even sitting for long periods of time in front of a computer can build up varying degrees of stress resulting in tight muscles and strained eyes. Get up every hour and walk around for at least five minutes. Some companies (Boeing, Cisco Systems, Unilever) offer employees biofeedback programs through which they hook up and check their heart rhythms to judge how they are handling stress during the work day. People then learn to take remedial action if their stress level has approached the "out of bounds" limit.

Even driving home can be terribly stressful depending on your usual route and the traffic you encounter. Bring along tapes or CD's and perhaps even study a foreign language—or call someone you care for on your cell phone (using headphones, not hand held receivers) and chat while in the traffic. In most cases, public transportation will be much less stressful than long road trips between work and home. I commuted by train for many years between New York City and a New Jersey suburb. While on the 40 minute train ride I napped, read, chatted with a friend, or meditated on the varying parts of my life. The stress of the day diminished and I could readily move into my home environment which might have included a Little League game, mediating an argument among children, attending a meeting of a local board, or just cutting the lawn or trimming the shrubs. In the evening while lounging in your robe and slippers, late night comedy re-runs are even better than hard news. Laughter stimulates blood flow which better fertilizes your entire body.

A sure way to learn to tolerate any situation is to get along with those around you. In the latter half of the 20th century, a syndicated pop psychologist using the name "Ann Landers" offered life style advice to many who wrote letters to her Post Office Box in Chicago. Ann Landers, born Esther Pauline Friedman of Russian immigrants, grew up in Sioux City, Iowa; married; and later moved to Chicago where she convinced a newspaper editor that she should replace an already functioning, but recently retired "Ann Landers" columnist in the local paper. The new "Ann" was an immediate hit and expanded her column through world wide syndication. She died at age 83 and 2002. In 1977 she had published what she called the "Ten Commandments of How to Get Along With People." In all of our day to day dealings with others, these tips can help us tolerate others and are guaranteed to help us get along much better with each other. Here is a synopsis of her Commandments.

1. Keep skid chains on your tongue; always say less than you think and cultivate a low, persuasive voice.
2. Make promises sparingly, but keep them faithfully, no matter what the cost.
3. Try and say a kind and encouraging word to others; praise good work and criticize helpfully.
4. Be interested in others—their joys and their sorrows-- and regard all others as persons of importance.
5. Be cheerful; don't dwell on your aches and pains with others; don't burden or depress others with any problems of yours.

6. Keep an open mind; discuss, but don't argue; disagree without being disagreeable.
7. Let your virtues, if you have any, speak for themselves.
8. Be careful of another's feelings; don't make jokes at the other's expense.
9. Pay no attention to ill-natured remarks about you. Simply live so that nobody will believe them.
10. Don't be too anxious about credit due you; do your best and be patient; let others remember you and your good works.

My friend, Gerial, (see Chapter 5) took a job in a newly-created Human Resources Department of a large and respected university complex where, unfortunately, the department executives had never heard of Ann Lander's Ten Commandments. They violated at least Commandments three, four, and six. Gerial was on a team charged with creating "a product," as she called it, to advise and train the university's managers in the basic techniques of management— hiring, training, performance rating, job placement, etc. Gerial's team created the "product" and it was poised for implementation, but before it was fully operational, Gerial resigned her position. Her tolerance level had been stretched to the breaking point by the executives the institution had employed— *all from the outside*— to manage her new team that was to create the new Human Resources "product" on how to manage people. These new and highly paid executives were woefully derelict in their own management skills. They were so over-confident, belligerent, and totally unable to mold their entire department into a solid, creative unit, that the work Gerial and her team accomplished in building a basic management "product" was never fully made operational. Over an eighteen month period, the staff of seventeen had 22 employee turnovers! This emphasized right up front that when certain conditions are so difficult, unstable, or otherwise miserable, tolerance must give way to termination. And that's just what Gerial did. She baled out and moved into a much better and more stimulating situation.

There's another story about a man who took a job that had all the markings of a good workplace, that is, until he actually began working there. No sooner had he started than he found himself in a culture that prized long hours only for the sake of long hours. Edicts from partners were urgent; projects needed revising six or seven times, but for no other reason than to satisfy the partners. If he wanted to leave on time and celebrate his wedding anniversary, forget it. Other family or personal celebrations—sorry. The man had no life of his own with this new job. He could not tolerate the stress, the unnecessary pressure, and the foolhardy expectations. So like many others locked in intolerable posts, he said "good-bye," walked out the door, and started his own business.

An op-ed piece in the *New York Times* by Serge Schmemann focused on *tolerance* in a very divided world. A statement in his editorial said, "to tolerate means little more than live and let live." Thus it is in a job situation. Can you live with the conditions surrounding you? Can you let others working with you live without interference from you or from others in the immediate environment? Schmemann wrote about tolerance in a universal sense that reaches out into a world much broader than employment. He was writing about the tolerance among all political or religious groups that make up modern society. Down through the ages, he pointed out that levels of tolerance varied widely, among religions especially. Even today, religious intolerance has been the primary element leading to wars, killings, and untold suffering. And we can ask this question which pertains both to society and to our workplaces: "Can one tolerate the wholly intolerant?" Most people would probably say, "no." What elements in our workplaces stretch our own abilities to tolerate? Most of us, in order to survive the corporate culture, would exit an intolerable situation. We would seek an environment where our working conditions are not over burdened and choked by situations that are difficult to tolerate.

LESSON XV: In your workplace, attempt to follow "Ann Landers" Ten Commandments in order to attempt to make your own working conditions tolerable. If you initiate positive interaction with your fellow employees, you will find that situations you thought were intolerable will dramatically improve.

Life can be playing games of stress with you in all facets of your existence. When your work environment is stressful, either soften the stress where you work, or walk out the door into the daylight of a more peaceful, more healthful, and less stressful existence.

CHAPTER SIXTEEN

PLANNING YOUR NEXT MOVE

While the thrust of this book is to help individuals survive the culture of their workplaces, almost everyone will somewhere, sometime, somehow, be thinking about another work venue— whether it will be a promotion in the present unit or department, transferring to a more promising locale within the same organization, or moving on and out, crossing to the potential "greener pastures." There are some large organizations that hire very carefully, hope to retain their staff and do most of their promoting from within. Other corporate entities consider long-term and loyal employment lower on their criteria of successful corporate stability.

Back in Chapter Two we discussed the old AT & T before the judicial breakup that created such a dramatic change in culture as the Bell System became fractured and split into competing parts. Under the old Bell structure, there was minimal turnover outside the system. People moved around within the system, moving from a local Bell company to a sister company or moving up into the parent AT & T, then sometimes back into the original Bell company at a new and higher lever position. There was little planning among employees for a move, and particularly those on a management track fully expected to have the big corporate wizard do the planning and the execution of job transfers and promotions.

The New Jersey suburb where I spent 26 years had a large sprinkling of residents who spent their entire careers within the Bell system—either at New Jersey Bell, New York Bell Telephone, or at the corporate headquarters of AT & T at 195 Broadway in New York City. During their long careers, they might move in and out of various Bell companies, but their lives were planned for them and they always knew that given acceptable performance, there would be jobs within the system. These carefully programmed careers would be followed by an attractive retirement package which usually included a decent pension supplemented by the dividends from the AT & T stock which they had been able to accumulate during their working years. It was a stable, steady, predictable career path, not littered with risk, land mines, or too much excitement. There was very little job related stress or trauma.

So looking at the possibilities of your next move, as we said—a promotion within your present unit, department, or team; a transfer to another operation in the same organization; or an escape (or even a friendly jump away from home) to a competitor or a totally new life style direction, here are some suggestions for all three possibilities.

FIRST—and most likely—a promotion within your own group: no matter what type of activity you are in, there are rules of performance to follow in order to be assured of promotion. These include:

• Be certain that your initial hire came with the blessing of your present boss and at least one more in the next level of management. If you have been thrust upon a reluctant supervisor, watch out. Your chances of being well received, much less promoted from within, are slim.
• Attend and become involved with whatever the required training, learning, course work, or licensing classes prepare you to function

well within your own unit. Don't be a smart-ass pupil; just apply yourself with vigor, without complaint, and perform well.

• Form that first alliance (see Chapter Five) with a more experienced person who is performing well in the operation. This person will not necessarily be the most popular person in the unit, but someone who knows how to succeed. You're looking for someone who performs well to the pleasure of the boss and who can mentor you to blend well with the accepted routines of the organization.

• Perform well, up to and somewhat above expectations.

As you progress in your work, you need to learn what promotion opportunities might become available. Some organizations promote for the wrong reasons. For example, a company I once worked for would reward their best sales persons with promotions into management. WRONG! Their skills produced superior sales results, but often unsuccessful management results. The new and failed managers often left the company or reverted back to sales, leaving a trail of frustration behind. Senior management soon learned that, rather than promotions, sales personnel responded best to more creative compensation packages rather than ill-timed management promotions. Assuming your organization promotes for the *right* reasons, become acquainted with various persons who have moved into positions to which you might aspire. Learn what their duties are, also their likes and dislikes about their jobs, and, more important, learn what *their* next moves might be. In a large organization, the promotion tracks may or may not be predictable, but they are very critical. In a small unit or a non-profit organization, there may be no promotion opportunities within that unit, so your choice is to stay where you are, enjoying and performing your work, or planning to use your talents elsewhere.

SECOND—Planning for an ultimate transfer to another operation within the same organization. This will be the most difficult, sensitive, politically challenging, and otherwise fraught with potential land mines of all the possible moves that can be made.

Before you make the first open gesture to effect such a transfer, ask these critical questions and don't request the transfer without having the answer to every last question.

• How are you perceived in your present position? Are you performing up to expectations? Would your record, written or oral, present the kind of message a new boss would receive with enthusiasm?
• Do you know persons in the projected new operation? Are they generally pleased with the work, their supervisor(s), their co-workers, the work environment, and the opportunities for advancement?
• How are the relations between your present boss and the one you hope to work for? Do they have a collegial and trusting relationship now, or are they involved with internal strife, competition, and other issues that might cast a negative pall over a possible transfer?
• How will requesting this transfer affect your future potential for continued growth within the organization? What has been the fate of others before you that have transferred between operations in this organization?
• Will your present boss endorse the move, even though it might weaken his/her staff— temporarily, we hope? Would a transfer from department one to department two be pleasant with a warm and jolly send-off, or will there be anger, jealousies, or resentment upon your departure?

All of these questions need answering, but even though all the answers might not provide the best possible comfort level, you might move ahead with the transfer request, depending on how many and which questions were answered in the negative. I once hired a young man during my first experience as a supervisor. He worked diligently and was a major asset to my operation. One day he appeared, saying he wished to chat about something. (Alarm bells always ring when you are approached in that manner.) We were in a home office administrative unit, serving the needs of people in the field sales organization. He fully stunned me. Not only did he wish to transfer to a department making and marketing a different product, he wanted to leave the home office and market this different product from a field office. What could I say? I endorsed the transfer, told *my* boss about his request, and after all the approvals from his new department were processed, we wished him well and sent him off. For this young man, the move presented new opportunities. He did well in the new operation and eventually left the firm and moved into an allied profession where his overall rewards and satisfaction levels exceeded his work with us.

Another friend of mine worked in a large New York City bank and had been moving along well in the bank's operations and saw an opening for his skills in another department that he felt offered more potential than his present position. He knew the proper manager in this new operation, so he spoke to her about an opening that might exist. The two of them had preliminary discussions and came to the conclusion that he would be ideal for a position that was about to open. The only problem was that the new manager-to-be and his present one were close friends, had been associates throughout their banking careers, and these secret behind-the-scenes negotiations were troublesome and caused some guilt feelings.

This whole transfer had been discussed quietly and only between the potential new manager and the would-be transferee. These were high-risk negotiations in the corporate world and could have led to charges and counter charges between two high-rising managers who had been long time friends and associates. As what transpired in this situation, sometimes it is essential to start behind-the-scenes negotiations with a future manager or department person of a potential new location, but these negotiations must be done very carefully to avoid negative repercussions on yourself and upon the person with whom you are negotiating. In this specific situation, the present manager endorsed the transfer and business relations among all parties remained cordial.

The least troublesome technique in arranging an inter-departmental transfer is to gather all the answers to the above questions, then begin to explore the possibilities with your present manager. You might start this exploration with some questions or conversational comments with your manager—"One of my friends, Tom, in Department X, says some real interesting developments are happening there." or "How do you think Department X is doing?—are they making their numbers?—how's the new manager doing there?" or "I hear Department X is moving to our new plant and manufacturing the new widgets we have been hearing about. That sounds exciting." These comments or questions will let your manager know that you have something up your sleeve regarding Department X and he/she will begin to ask you questions as to why this conversation about Department X. It's then that you can casually mention a possible transfer to that department. Keep the conversation casual until you get whatever message your manager is sending back to you. If you're getting a defensive and disturbed response, drop the subject, to be brought up another day under different conditions. If your manager seems interested in discussing a possible transfer, have your reasons ready and try to keep the conversation moving. It's a known fact that once a decision to move has been made, it's pointless to assume any further productivity in the old location. Move the process along as fast as possible so you'll be moved into Department X and ready to perform in record time. Your old manager will be sorry to lose you, but if the transfer request was handled with dignity and with honest intentions to leave on good terms, the transfer should go smoothly and swiftly.

THIRD—Seeking a new job in a new organization. This can be the most fun and offers multiple opportunities to make the correct connection. I had a glorious adventure when I sought the very last job I had prior to opening my own business. I had worked for a semi-large international insurance broker, Corroon & Black of New York (later merged into The Willis Group) and had recently been caught in a management shuffle which allowed me to remain there, but with less responsibility and authority. My goal was to move to the world's largest firm of this type, Marsh & McLennan. Down the street from my home in New Jersey lived a retired, but very senior executive, of Guy Carpenter Company, the international and wholly owned reinsurance affiliate of Marsh. I stopped by to see him and told him I wanted an introduction to Mr. X, another very senior executive of Marsh who also lived in my town. This worked out very smoothly. Mr. X called me and invited me to lunch in his New York City club. We had several martini's, a good discussion during which he discovered, to his delight, that I had broker control of a Corroon & Black account that he had coveted for some time. We immediately made plans for further interviews with several executives at Marsh. When the final gun went off, I was hired to do exactly what I wanted to do, eventually brought the coveted account into the company and had several productive years with my new employer. Eventually, however, I left Marsh to start my own business and was able to continue the relationship with the coveted account on my own.

As this story will testify, personal contacts are the most ideal means to move from one organization to another. That is why I had instructed readers earlier in this book to make alliances with individuals in other firms whenever the opportunity arises. While my contact to arrange the job described above was a personal neighborly friendship, any positive connection will do.

Obviously, another successful technique is to follow the careers of those with whom you have worked and who have moved on to new positions. They will have information and connections within their organizations to assist you—if you feel there are opportunities that appeal to you. Your friends there should give you honest assessments of job opportunities and employment conditions so that you have accurate information if and when you start the interviewing process.

Employment agencies, help wanted ads, and executive search firms are the big, professional job search media in this country. My office in New York has had good success seeking administrative and clerical employees through the *New York Times* newspaper help wanted section. The cost is minimal and the *Times* is usually read by individuals who are likely qualified for the open positions. I once was employed by a firm who found me through an employment agency. My employer was required to pay the employment agency fee, which usually is quite substantial, and even though I was the chosen person, my employer complained for years about the fee paid to find me.

At one time I was disenchanted with my present employment and began searching around for something more satisfying. I had not built adequate alliances, so I decided to sign up with a search firm that required an up front fee from me, the candidate. After tests, several unsatisfactory interviews, and months of delays, the search firm itself went bankrupt. I lost my entire fee, had no decent job opportunities, and was back to square one. My advice to anyone who plans to enroll with a firm requiring an up front fee—DON'T! Employment agencies and search firms are paid for performance—that means, paid after a placement has taken place. True, some of the larger search firms trading in high level positions might demand a retainer fee, but this is never paid by a job candidate. It is always paid by the organization initiating the search.

Executive search firms normally are retained by employers to search for qualified persons to fill generally high level positions. When Carly Fiorina was found and employed by Hewlett Packard, you can rest assured that the firm that did the search received a large chunk of money for the job.

During the earlier years of my career when I was potential job bait for other companies, I had several interviews set up by search firms operating for major clients. I once was called to look at a position to be the marketing officer for Blue Cross of Wisconsin. I flew from New York to Milwaukee for the interview and met with the President of the firm. He was known as a fast moving dynamo who worked around the clock, traveling from city to city in Wisconsin to keep his Blue Cross plan meeting its objectives. He expected the new marketing executive to follow the same schedule. When I told him I had a family, including three children, that I spent time working with the Boy Scouts and my local church, he decided quickly that I would never be the 100% dedicated Blue Cross executive he sought. The interview ended quickly. A friend of mine eventually was hired for this job and had an early heart attack attempting to keep up with the excessive job requirements. I had a similar interview arranged by a head hunter with Maurice "Hank" Greenburg, Chairman and CEO of American International Group, a large international insurance organization based in New York. I was being interviewed for a job managing the marketing of group insurance to firms located in Europe and Asia—something I knew absolutely nothing about. The interview was brief.

Good search firms would not have included me in the interview process for either of these jobs. I didn't fit the requirements or the culture of either position, although they would have been many steps up from where I was with substantial pay increases. If you have a position of any stature, you will be solicited by search firms who need names of potential executives. They may be looking for you. They may be scratching around for other names. My advice is to treat them courteously but warily. There job is to complete a search and the sooner they do it, the sooner they will receive their fee. There are many search firms that are very reputable and highly professional, and if you get calls from any, check them out with your associates, check them out on the internet, and if they appear ethical and professional, deal with them on an equally professional manner. Otherwise, thank them politely and wait for another call.

LESSON XVI: If you hope to move within your organization, whether in your present department or to a totally separate and different operation of the same organization, the first rule is to be performing well where you are. Some managers would be happy to "dump" a poor performer, but finding a taker would be tough. If your present manager can testify to good performance, the manager of the coveted spot will be more willing to accept the transferee.

As we have said throughout this book, alliances will help satisfy many corporate needs. Alliances within your operation or organization will, second to satisfactory performance, almost guarantee you the move, promotion, or new responsibility that you seek. But have complete answers to the five questions above, whether or not you base your action on full and satisfactory answers to the questions.

Looking for work outside your organization can by fun, challenging, and will open you to fresh ways of functioning. Before jumping off your ship into the neighboring luxury liner, do a thorough intelligence search of the new organization, including its financial stability, employee turnover ratio, and the opportunities for advancing your career on better terms than at your present shop.

NEVER ENTER INTO ANY CORPORATE COMMUNITY OR EMPLOYEE/EMPLOYER RELATIONSHIP WITHOUT PERSONAL RESEARCH, INCLUDING ASKING LOTS OF QUESTIONS OF PEOPLE WHO WOULD KNOW THE ANSWERS. IN YOUR EFFORT TO SURVIVE (OR ESCAPE), HAVE FRIENDS THAT CAN HELP IN EITHER CASE. YOUR OWN EMPLOYMENT WELFARE COMES FIRST; DON'T SELL YOUR CAREER OR YOUR JOBS DOWN THE RIVER BY IGNORING THE LESSONS YOU HAVE HAD AN OPPORTUNITY TO LEARN.